Cram101 Textbook Outlines to accompany:

Racial and Ethnic Groups

Schaefer, 10th Edition

A Cram101 Inc. publication (c) 2009.

PRACTICE EXAMS.

Get all of the self-teaching practice exams for each chapter of this textbook at **www.Cram101.com** and ace the tests. Here is an example:

Chapter 1

Racial and Ethnic Groups
Schaefer, 10th Edition,
All Material Written and Prepared by Cram101

I WANT A BETTER GRADE.   Items 1 - 50 of 100. ▶

1 _____ was an American anthropologist. A prolific writer, he was highly influential in the development of cultural materialism. In his work he combined Karl Marx's emphasis on the forces of production with Malthus's insights on the impact of demographic factors on other parts of the sociocultural system. Labeling demographic and production factors as infrastructure, Harris posited these factors as key in determining a society's social structure and culture.

⚪ Marvin Harris   ⚪ M. Arnold
⚪ M. Banim   ⚪ M. Callon

2 _____ is a word used in several official titles of various branches of society. As they became trusted members of the courts of Medieval Europe, the title grew in reputation. During the last few centuries, it has been used for the most elevated offices.

⚪ Marshal   ⚪ M. Arnold
⚪ M. Banim   ⚪ M. Callon

3 An _____ is a population of human beings whose members identify with each other, usually on the basis of a presumed common genealogy or ancestry. Ethnicity is also defined from the recognition by others as a distinct group and by common cultural, linguistic, religious, behavioral or biological traits.

⚪ Ethnic group   ⚪ E.F. Hutton & Co.
⚪ Early onset   ⚪ Early-later experience issue

4 In sociology, a group can be defined as two or more humans that interact with one another, accept expectations

With Cram101.com online, you also have access to extensive reference material.

You will nail those essays and papers. Here is an example from a Cram101 Biology text:

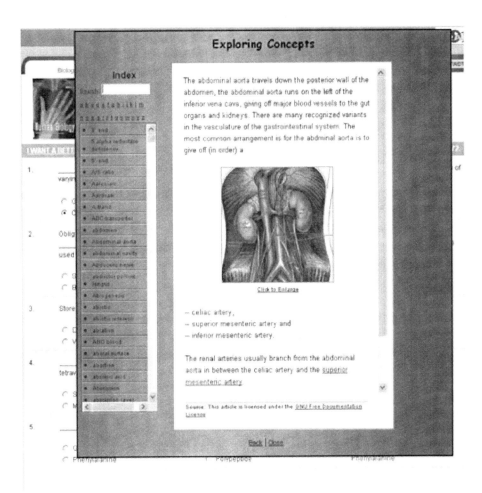

Visit **www.Cram101.com**, click Sign Up at the top of the screen, and enter DK73DW4426 in the promo code box on the registration screen. Access to www.Cram101.com is normally $9.95 per month, but because you have purchased this book, your access fee is only $4.95 per month, cancel at any time. Sign up and stop highlighting textbooks forever.

Learning System

Cram101 Textbook Outlines is a learning system. The notes in this book are the highlights of your textbook, you will never have to highlight a book again.

How to use this book. Take this book to class, it is your notebook for the lecture. The notes and highlights on the left hand side of the pages follow the outline and order of the textbook. All you have to do is follow along while your instructor presents the lecture. Circle the items emphasized in class and add other important information on the right side. With Cram101 Textbook Outlines you'll spend less time writing and more time listening. Learning becomes more efficient.

Cram101.com Online

Increase your studying efficiency by using Cram101.com's practice tests and online reference material. It is the perfect complement to Cram101 Textbook Outlines. Use self-teaching matching tests or simulate in-class testing with comprehensive multiple choice tests, or simply use Cram's true and false tests for quick review. Cram101.com even allows you to enter your in-class notes for an integrated studying format combining the textbook notes with your class notes.

Visit **www.Cram101.com**, click Sign Up at the top of the screen, and enter **DK73DW4426** in the promo code box on the registration screen. Access to www.Cram101.com is normally $9.95, but because you have purchased this book, your access fee is only $4.95. Sign up and stop highlighting textbooks forever.

Racial and Ethnic Groups
Schaefer, 10th

CONTENTS

Marvin Harris	Marvin Harris was an American anthropologist. A prolific writer, he was highly influential in the development of cultural materialism. In his work he combined Karl Marx's emphasis on the forces of production with Malthus's insights on the impact of demographic factors on other parts of the sociocultural system. Labeling demographic and production factors as infrastructure, Harris posited these factors as key in determining a society's social structure and culture.
Marshal	Marshal is a word used in several official titles of various branches of society. As they became trusted members of the courts of Medieval Europe, the title grew in reputation. During the last few centuries, it has been used for the most elevated offices.
Ethnic group	An ethnic group is a population of human beings whose members identify with each other, usually on the basis of a presumed common genealogy or ancestry. Ethnicity is also defined from the recognition by others as a distinct group and by common cultural, linguistic, religious, behavioral or biological traits.
Groups	In sociology, a group can be defined as two or more humans that interact with one another, accept expectations and obligations as members of the group, and share a common identity. By this definition, society can be viewed as a large group, though most social groups are considerably smaller.
Military	Military has two broad meanings. In its first sense, it refers to soldiers and soldiering. In its second sense, it refers to armed forces as a whole.
Status	In sociology or anthropology, social status is the honor or prestige attached to one's position in society one's social position. The stratification system, which is the system of distributing rewards to the members of society, determines social status. Social status, the position or rank of a person or group within the stratification system, can be determined two ways. One can earn their social status by their own achievements, which is known as achieved status, or one can be placed in the stratification system by their inherited position, which is called ascribed status.
Majority	A majority is a subset of a group that is more than half of the entire group.
Dominance	In animal colonies, a condition established by one animal over another by prevailing in an aggressive encounter between the two, is referred to as dominance.
William Graham Sumner	William Graham Sumner an American academic and professor at Yale College. He was a polymath with numerous books and essays on American history, economic history, political theory, sociology, and anthropology. His popular essays gave him a wide audience for his laissez-faire: advocacy of free markets, anti-imperialism, and the gold standard.
Ethnicity	Ethnicity is a population of human beings whose members identify with each other, either on the basis of a presumed common genealogy or ancestry or recognition by others as a distinct group, or by common cultural, linguistic, religious, or physical traits. The sociologist Max Weber once remarked that "The whole conception of it is so complex and so vague that it might be good to abandon it altogether."
Population	A population is the collection of people or organisms of a particular species living in a given geographic area or space, usually measured by a census.
Race	The term race refers to the concept of dividing people into populations or groups on the basis of various sets of characteristics and beliefs about common ancestry. The most widely used human racial categories are based on visible traits especially skin color, facial features and hair texture, and self-identification.
Cultural diversity	Cultural diversity is the variety of human societies or cultures in a specific region, or in the world as a whole.
Minority	A minority is a sociological group that does not constitute a politically dominant plurality of the total population of a given society. A sociological minority is not necessarily a numerical minority

Go to **Cram101.com** for the Practice Tests for this Chapter.
And, **NEVER** highlight a book again!

	it may include any group that is disadvantaged with respect to a dominant group in terms of social status, education, employment, wealth and political power.
Religious group	A religious group is a subgroup within a religion that operates under a common name, tradition, and identity.
Workplace	A workplace is any plant, yard, premises, room or other vicinity where employees engage in the performance of labor or service over which an employer has the right of access and control.
Bell Curve	The Bell Curve is a controversial, best-selling book by the late Harvard professor Richard J. Herrnstein and American Enterprise Institute political pundit Charles Murray. Its central point is that intelligence is a better predictor of many factors including financial income, job performance, unwed pregnancy, and crime than parent's Socio-Economic status or education level.
Cultural bias	Cultural bias refers to a factor that provides an advantage for test takers from certain cultural or ethnic backgrounds, such as using test items that are based on middle-class culture in the United States.
Richard Herrnstein	Richard Herrnstein was a prominent researcher in animal learning in the Skinnerian tradition. He was one of the founders of Quantitative Analysis of Behavior. His major research finding as an experimental psychologist is called "Matching law" -- the tendency of animals to allocate their choices in direct proportion to the rewards they provide.
Human	Human beings are bipedal primates in the family Hominidae. DNA evidence indicates that modern humans originated in Africa about 250,000 years ago. Humans have a highly developed brain, capable of abstract reasoning, language, introspection, and emotion. This mental capability, combined with an erect body carriage that frees the forelimbs for manipulating objects, has allowed humans to make far greater use of tools than any other species. Humans now permanently inhabit every continent on Earth, except Antarctica. Humans also now have a continuous presence in low Earth orbit, occupying the International Space Station. The human population on Earth amounts to over 6.7 billion, as of July, 2008.
Human Genome Project	The Human Genome Project is a project undertaken with a goal to understand the genetic make-up of the human species by determining the DNA sequence of the human genome and the genome of a few model organisms. Most of the genome DNA sequencing for the Human Genome Project was done by researchers at universities and research centers in the the United States and Great Britain, with other genome DNA sequencing done independently by the private company Celera Genomics.
Intelligence	Intelligence is a property of mind that encompasses many related abilities, such as the capacities to reason, to plan, to solve problems, to think abstractly, to comprehend ideas, to use language, and to learn. In some cases, intelligence may include traits such as: creativity, personality, character, knowledge, or wisdom.
Marriage	A marriage is an interpersonal relationship with governmental, social, or religious recognition, usually intimate and sexual, and often created as a contract. The most frequently occurring form of marriage unites a man and a woman as husband and wife. Other forms of marriage also exist; for example, polygamy, in which a person takes more than one spouse, is common in many societies
Bias	A bias is a prejudice in a general or specific sense, usually in the sense for having a preference to one particular point of view or ideological perspective.
Controversy	A controversy is a matter of opinion over which parties actively disagree, argue, or debate. Controversies can range in size from private disputes between two individuals to large-scale disagreements between societies.
Apartheid	Apartheid was a system of racial segregation in South Africa. The rules of Apartheid dictated that people be legally classified into racial groups -- the main ones were Black, White, Coloured and Indian -- and separated from one another on the basis of legal classification and unequal rights.

Winston Churchill	Winston Churchill was a British politician known chiefly for his leadership of the United Kingdom during World War II. He served as Prime Minister of the United Kingdom from 1940 to 1945 and again from 1951 to 1955. A noted statesman and orator, Churchill was also an officer in the British Army, a historian, a Nobel Prize-winning writer, and an artist.
Ashley Montagu	Ashley Montagu, was a British-American anthropologist and humanist who popularized issues such as race and gender and their relation to politics and development. He was the rapporteur, in 1950, of the UNESCO statement The Race Question.
Racism	Racism, by its simplest definition, is discrimination based on race. People with racist beliefs might hate certain groups of people according to their race, or in the case of institutional racism, certain racial groups may be denied rights or benefits. Racism typically starts with the assumption that there are taxonomic differences between different groups of people. According to the United Nations conventions, there is no distinction between the term racial discrimination and ethnic discrimination.
Social construction	A social construction is an institutionalized entity or artifact in a social system 'invented' or 'constructed' by participants in a particular culture or society that exists solely because people agree to behave as if it exists, or agree to follow certain conventional rules.
Genocide	Genocide is the deliberate and systematic destruction of an ethnic, religious or national group. It is define as "any of the following acts committed with intent to destroy, in whole or in part, a national, ethnical, racial or religious group, as such: killing members of the group; causing serious bodily or mental harm to members of the group; deliberately inflicting on the group conditions of life, calculated to bring about its physical destruction in whole or in part; imposing measures intended to prevent births within the group; forcibly transferring children of the group to another group."
Hans Gerth	Hans Gerth was a scholar and translator of major works into English. He is perhaps best known for translating all of Max Weber's works during World War II, due to being placed under house arrest. He died at the age of 70 in Frankfort, West Germany in 1979.
Mills	Mills is best remembered for studying the structure of Power in the U.S. in his book, The Power Elite. Mills was concerned with the responsibilities of intellectuals in post-World War II society, and advocated relevance and engagement over disinterested academic observation, as a "public intelligence apparatus" in challenging the crackpot policies of these institutional elite in the "Big Three", the economic, political and military.
C. Wright Mills	C. Wright Mills was an American sociologist. Mills is best remembered for studying the structure of power in the U.S. in his book The Power Elite. Mills was concerned with the responsibilities of intellectuals in post-World War II society, and advocated relevance and engagement over disinterested academic observation, as a "public intelligence apparatus" in challenging the policies of the institutional elites in the "Three" the economic, political and military.
Michael Omi	Michael Omi is an American sociologist. Professor Omi is most well known for developing the theory of racial formation along with Howard Winant. Omi serves on the faculty at the University of California, Berkeley. Omi's work includes race theory, Asian American studies, and antiracist scholarship.
Racial formation	Racial formation is an analytical theory developed by Michael Omi and Howard Winant which is used to look at race as a socially constructed identity, where the content and importance of racial categories is determined by social, economic, and political forces. Unlike other traditional race theories, In Omi and Winant's view, racial meanings pervade US society, extending from the shaping of individual racial identities to the structuring of collective political action on the terrain of the state.
Stratification	Stratification is the hierarchical arrangement of social classes, castes, and strata within a society. While these hierarchies are not universal to all societies, they are the norm among state-

Go to **Cram101.com** for the Practice Tests for this Chapter.

	level cultures.
Max weber	Max Weber was a German political economist and sociologist who is considered one of the founders of the modern study of sociology and public administration. His major works deal with rationalisation in sociology of religion and government, but he also contributed much in the field of economics. His most famous work is his essay The Protestant Ethic and the Spirit of Capitalism, which began his work in the sociology of religion.
Howard Winant	Howard Winant is an American sociologist and race theorist. Professor Winant is most well known for developing the theory of racial formation along with Michael Omi. Currently, Winant is Professor of Sociology at the University of California, Santa Barbara. Winant's research and teachings revolve around race and racism, comparative historical sociology, political sociology, social theory, and human rights.
Gender	Gender refers to the differences between men and women. Gender identity is an individual's self-conception as being male or female, as distinguished from actual biological sex. In general, gender often refers to purely social rather than biological differences.
Sociology	Sociology is the scientific or systematic study of society, including patterns of social relationships, social interaction, and culture. Areas studied in sociology can range from the analysis of brief contacts between anonymous individuals on the street to the study of global social interaction. Numerous fields within the discipline concentrate on how and why people are organized in society, either as individuals or as members of associations, groups, and institutions. Sociology is considered a branch of social science.
Functionalism	In the social sciences, specifically sociology and sociocultural anthropology, functionalism is a sociological paradigm that originally attempted to explain social institutions as collective means to fill individual biological needs.
Functionalist perspective	Functionalist perspective is a sociological viewpoint that argues that social inequality is necessary for the survival of any society or for any small or large organization. It is argued that without this inequality, division labor would be difficult.
Comparable worth	The evaluation of jobs dominated by women and those traditionally dominated by men on the basis of training, skills, and experience in attempts to equalize wage is referred to as comparable worth.
Conflict perspective	A theoretical perspective that focuses on the struggle among different social groups over scarce resources is referred to as conflict perspective or conflict theory.
Dysfunction	Dysfunction refers to an institution's negative impact on the sociocultural system.
Joe R. Feagin	Joe R. Feagin is a U.S. sociologist and social theorist who has conducted extensive research on racial and gender issues, especially in regard to the United States. Joe R. Feagin along with Jessie Daniels launched Racism Review a website designed to provide a credible and reliable source of information "race," racism, ethnicity, and immigration issues, especially as they undergird and shape U.S. society within a global setting.
Pay equity	Pay equity is a method of eliminating discrimination against women who are paid less than men for jobs requiring comparable levels of expertise. A policy to establish pay equity usuallys refers to that all jobs will be evaluated and given points according to the level of knowledge and responsibility required to do the job and that salary adjustments will be made if its discovered that women are consistently paid less then men for jobs with similar points.
Equity	Equity is the concept or idea of fairness in economics, particularly as to taxation or welfare economics.
American Dilemma	An American Dilemma: The Negro Problem and Modern Democracy is a 1944 study of race relations authored by Swedish economist Gunnar Myrdal and funded by The Carnegie Foundation. The foundation chose Myrdal because it thought that as a non-American, he could offer a more unbiased opinion.

Go to **Cram101.com** for the Practice Tests for this Chapter.

Myrdal's volume, at nearly 1,500 pages, painstakingly detailed what he saw as obstacles to full participation in American society that were faced by African-Americans as of the 1940s. It sold over 100,000 copies and went through 25 printings before going into its second edition in 1965. It was enormously influential in how racial issues were viewed in the United States, and it was cited in the landmark Brown v. Board case "in general." The book was generally positive in its outlook on the future of race relations in America, taking the view that democracy would triumph over racism. In many ways it laid the groundwork for future policies of racial integration and affirmative action.

Blame	To blame is to hold another person or group responsible for perceived faults real, imagined, or merely invented for pejorative purposes.
Arlie Russell Hochschild	Arlie Russell Hochschild is a professor of sociology at the University of California, Berkeley. She is the author of several prize-winning books and numerous articles which discuss the dual labor by women in both the general economy and within the household. In her essay, "Love and Gold" in Global Woman: Nannies, Maids and Sex Workers in the New Economy, she sets the concept of emotional labor in a larger political context.
Labeling	Labeling is defining or describing a person in terms of his or her behavior. The term is often used in sociology to describe human interaction, control and identification of deviant behavior.
Labeling theory	A social theory that holds that society's reaction to certain behaviors is a major factor in defining the self as deviant is labeling theory.
Myrdal, Gunnar	Myrdal, Gunnar was a Swedish economist and politician. He, along with Friedrich von Hayek, won the Nobel Prize for Economics for their "pioneering work in the theory of money and economic fluctuations and for their penetrating analysis of the interdependence of economic, social and institutional phenomena." He was also known for his study, An American Dilemma: The Negro Problem and Modern Democracy, which influenced the US Supreme Court decision in Brown v. Board of Education to outlaw racial segregation in public schools.
Self-fulfilling prophecy	A self-fulfilling prophecy is a prediction that directly or indirectly causes itself to become true. Sociologist Robert K. Merton who is credited with coining the expression "self-fulfilling prophecy" and formalizing its structure and consequences. He gives as a feature of the self-fulfilling prophecy: The self-fulfilling prophecy is, in the beginning, a true definition of the situation evoking a new behavior which makes the original false conception come 'true'.
William Isaac Thomas	William Isaac Thomas, was an American sociologist. He is noted for his pioneering work on the sociology of migration on which he co-operated with Florian Znaniecki, and for his formulation of what became known as the Thomas theorem, a fundamental law of sociology: "If men define situations as real, they are real in their consequences".
Minority group	A minority group or subordinate group is a sociological group that does not constitute a politically dominant plurality of the total population of a given society.
Sociological research	Sociological research refers to research conducted by social scientist. Before the advent of sociology and application of the scientific method to sociological research, human inquiry was mostly based on personal experiences, and received wisdom in the form of tradition and authority. Such approaches often led to errors such as inaccurate observations, overgeneralisation, selective observations, subjectivity and lack of logic.
Emigration	Emigration is the act and the phenomenon of leaving one's native country to settle abroad.
Migration	The movement of people from one country or region to another in order to settle permanently, is referred to as a migration.
Annexation	Annexation is the legal incorporation of some territory into another geo-political entity either adjacent or non-contiguous. Usually, it is implied that the territory and population being annexed is the smaller, more peripheral, and weaker of the two merging entities. It can also imply a certain measure of coercion, expansionism or unilateralism on the part of the stronger of the merging

	entities. Because of this, more positive terms like political union or reunification are sometimes preferred.
Derrick Bell	Derrick Bell is a visiting professor of Constitutional Law at New York University School of Law for the past years and a major figure within the legal studies discipline of Critical Race Theory.
Colonialism	Colonialism is the extension of a nation's sovereignty over territory beyond its borders by the establishment of either settler colonies or administrative dependencies in which indigenous populations are directly ruled or displaced.
Globalization	Globalization refers to increasing global connectivity, integration and interdependence in the economic, social, technological, cultural, political, and ecological spheres. It is a unitary process inclusive of many sub-processes that are increasingly binding people and the biosphere more tightly into one global system.
Mexican-American War	The Mexican-American War was an armed military conflict between the United States and Mexico in the wake of the U.S. annexation of Texas. The most important consequence of the war for the United States was the Mexican Cession, in which the Mexican territories of Alta California and Santa Fé de Nuevo México were ceded to the United States under the terms of the Treaty of Guadalupe Hidalgo. In Mexico, the enormous loss of territory following the war encouraged its government to enact policies to colonize its northern territories as a hedge against further losses.
Treaty of Guadalupe Hidalgo	The Treaty of Guadalupe Hidalgo is the peace treaty, largely dictated by the United States to the interim government of a militarily occupied Mexico, that ended the Mexican-American War.
Robert Blauner	Robert Blauner is an American college professor, author and sociologist. His well-known "Blauner Hypothesis" states that minority groups created by colonization, because it is forced on them, experience a greater degree of racism and discrimination than those created by voluntary immigration.
Internal colonialism	Internal Colonialism refers to political and economic inequalities between regions within a single society. The term may be used to describe the uneven effects of state development on a regional basis and to describe the exploitation of minority groups within the wider society.
Immanuel Wallerstein	Immanuel Wallerstein is a United States sociologist. He rejected the notion of a "Third World", claiming there was only one world connected by a complex network of economic exchange relationships, in which the 'dichotomy of capital and labor', and the endless 'accumulation of capital' by competing agents account for frictions. This approach is known as the World Systems Theory.
Oppression	Oppression is the negative outcome experienced by people targeted by the cruel exercise of power in a society or social group. It is particularly closely associated with nationalism and derived social systems, wherein identity is built by antagonism to the other.
Systems theory	A theory that emphasizes the interdependence of family members and how they affect one another is a systems theory.
Daniel Chirot	Daniel Chirot is Professor of International Studies and Sociology at the University of Washington. He specializes in ethnic conflict, social change, and tyranny. He has authored several influential books on Eastern Europe, social change in the modern era, and the nature of tyranny. He also consults with CARE in Africa, where he has worked in Niger and Cote d'Ivoire.
Ethnic cleansing	Ethnic cleansing refers to the creation of ethnically homogeneous territories through the mass expulsion of other ethnic populations.
Extermination	Extermination is the act of killing or murdering with the intention of eradicating demographics within a population.
Holocaust	The Holocaust is the term generally used to describe the killing of approximately six million European Jews during World War II, as part of a program of deliberate extermination planned and

executed by the National Socialist regime in Germany led by Adolf Hitler.

Rwanda	Yoweri Museveni's guerrilla forces in Uganda had succeeded in taking control of Rwanda, overthrowing the Ugandan dictatorship of Milton Obote. This conflict spilled over the border into Rwanda and caused the fragile Rwandan Arusha accords to quickly crumble. Tutsi-Hutu hatred rapidly intensified. Rwanda today struggles to heal and rebuild, but shows signs of rapid development. Some continue to grapple with the legacy of almost 60 years of intermittent war.
Secession	Secession is the act of withdrawing from an organization, union, or especially a political entity. It is not to be confused with succession, the act of following in order or sequence.
Vietnam	Vietnam is the easternmost country on the Indochina Peninsula in Southeast Asia. It is bordered by China to the north, Laos to the northwest, Cambodia to the southwest, and the South China Sea to the east. With a population of over 85 million, Vietnam is the 13th most populous country in the world.
Black Muslims	The term Black Muslim is widely credited to C. Eric Lincoln's 1961 book, The Black Muslims In America, which analyzed the growing influence of the Nation of Islam in the United States of America. The phrase is often used in the United States to denote members of Louis Farrakhan's separatist Black nationalist movement, the Nation of Islam. The Nation of Islam never appreciated being labeled "Black Muslims" and years afterward publicly denounced the title but as Malcolm X stated, "the name stuck." Today, the vast majority of Muslims in the African Diaspora are not members of the Nation of Islam. Rather, they follow local religious leaders who may or may not be Black, such as Siraj Wahaj, and worship at their local mosques.
Colonization	Colonization occurs whenever any one or more species populates a new area. The term, which is derived from the Latin colere, "to inhabit, cultivate, frequent, practice, tend, guard, respect," originally related to humans. However, 19th century biogeographers dominated the term to describe the activities of birds or bacteria, or plant species. Human colonization is a narrower category than the related concept of colonialism, because whereas colonization refers to the establishment of settler colonies, trading posts, and plantations with the metropole's own population, colonialism deals with this and the ruling of new territories' existing peoples.
Islam	Islam is a monotheistic religion originating with the teachings of Muhammad, a 7th-century Arab religious and political figure. Islam includes many religious practices. Adherents are generally required to observe the Five Pillars of Islam, which are five duties that unite Muslims into a community.
Liberia	Liberia is a country on the west coast of Africa, bordered by Sierra Leone, Guinea, Côte d'Ivoire, and the Atlantic Ocean. Liberia made a commitment to abolish capital punishment. A new law on rape, which initially proposed imposition of the death penalty for gang rape, was amended to provide a maximum penalty of life imprisonment." Liberia has a dual system of statutory law based on Anglo-American common law for the modern sector and customary unwritten law for the native sector for exclusively rural tribes.
Muslim	A Muslim is an adherent of the religion of Islam. They believe that there is only one God, translated in Arabic as Allah. They also believe that Islam existed long before Muhammad and that the religion has evolved with time.
Nation of Islam	The original Nation of Islam was founded in Detroit, Michigan in 1930 by Wallace Fard Muhammad also known as Master W. D. Fard Muhammad. The Nation of Islam teaches that W. Fard Muhammad is both the "Messiah" of Christianity and the Mahdi of Islam. One of Fard's first disciples was Elijah Muhammad, who led the organization from 1935 through 1975.
Segregation	Segregation may be mandated by law or exist through social norms. Segregation may be maintained by means ranging from discrimination in hiring and in the rental and sale of housing to certain races to vigilante violence such as lynchings; a situation that arises when members of different races mutually prefer to associate and do business with members of their own race would usually be described as separation or de facto separation of the races rather than segregation.

Go to **Cram101.com** for the Practice Tests for this Chapter.

Society	A society is a grouping of individuals, which is characterized by common interest and may have distinctive culture and institutions.
Census	A census is the process of obtaining information about every member of a population. It can be contrasted with sampling in which information is only obtained from a subset of a population. As such it is a method used for accumulating statistical data, and it is also vital to democracy.
Amalgamation	Amalgamation is a now largely archaic term for the intermarriage and interbreeding of different ethnicities or races. In the English-speaking world, the term has been in use into the twentieth century. In the United States, it was partly replaced after 1863 by the term miscegenation. While the term amalgamation could refer to the interbreeding of different white as well as non-white ethnicities, the term miscegenation was used to refer specifically to the interbreeding of whites and non-whites, especially African-Americans.[1]
Melting pot	The melting pot is a metaphor for the way in which homogeneous societies develop, in which the ingredients in the pot (people of different cultures and religions) are combined so as to lose their discrete identities to some degree, yielding a final product which has a more uniform consistency and flavor, and which is quite different from the original inputs.
Cannabis	Cannabis is a genus of flowering plants that includes three putative species, Cannabis sativa L., Cannabis indica Lam., and Cannabis ruderalis Janisch. These three taxa are indigenous to central Asia and surrounding regions. Cannabis has long been used for fibre, for medicinal purposes, and as a psychoactive.
Dominant group	The opposite of minority group, that possesses more wealth, power, and prestige in a society is a dominant group.
Charles Hirschman	Charles Hirschman is Professor of Sociology at the University of Washington. His areas of expertise are demography and ecology, immigration and ethnicity, fertility and family, social stratification and mobility, and Southeast Asia. He also directs the Univesity of Washington-Beyond High School project, a study of educational attainment and the early life course of young adults.
Assimilation	A minority group's internalization of the values and norms of the dominant culture is referred to as assimilation.
Resistance	Psychological resistance is the phenomenon often encountered in clinical practice in which patients either directly or indirectly oppose changing their behavior or refuse to discuss, remember, or think about presumably clinically relevant experiences.
Pluralism	Pluralism is, in the general sense, the affirmation and acceptance of diversity. Pluralism is connected with the hope that this process of conflict and dialogue will lead to a definition and subsequent realization of the common good that is best for all members of society.
Leo Srole	Leo Srole was a distinguished sociologist who directed landmark studies on the mental health of urban Americans. He drew widespread attention with his 1962 findings that only 18.5 of 1,660 New York City residents studied were in good mental health. His books included Mental Health in the Metropolis, and The Social Systems of American Ethnic Groups.
Tiger Woods	Tiger Woods whose achievements to date rank him among the most successful golfers of all time. Currently the World No. 1, Woods was the highest-paid professional athlete in 2007, having earned an estimated $122 million from winnings and endorsements. According to Golf Digest, Woods made $769,440,709 from 1996 to 2007, and the magazine predicts that by 2010, Woods will become the world's first athlete to pass one billion dollars in earnings.
City	A city is an urban area with a large population and a particular administrative, legal, or historical status.
Multiracial	The term multiracial describe people who are not easily classified into a single race. This has caused some problems for census-takers, until recently.

Double consciousness	Double consciousness, in its contemporary sense, is a term coined by W. E. B. Du Bois. The term is used to describe an individual whose identity is divided into several facets.
Yen Le Espiritu	Yen Le Espiritu is Professor and Chair of the Department of Ethnic Studies. She specializes in U.S. imperialism and wars, Southeast Asian refugees, and Filipino American history. She is interested on the transnational and gendered lives of Filipino immigrants and Filipino Americans.
Hispanic	Hispanic is a term that historically denoted relation to the ancient Hispania and its peoples. The term now refers to the culture and people of the Spanish-speaking countries of Hispanic America and Spain; or countries with a historical legacy from Spain, including the Southwestern United States and Florida; the African nations of Equatorial Guinea, Western Sahara and the Northern coastal region of Morocco; the Asia-Pacific nations of the Philippines, Guam, Northern Mariana Islands; and to the ethnic individuals of those cultures. It can also refer to the Hispanosphere geographical distribution, the same way Latin refers to the Romance languages in general.
Hispanic American	Hispanic American is an American citizen or resident of Hispanic ethnicity and can identify themselves as having Hispanic Cultural heritage. According to the 2000 Census, Hispanics constitute the second largest ethnic group in the United States, compromizing roughly 12.5% of the population.
Park	A park is a bounded area of land, usually in its natural or semi-natural landscaped state and set aside for some purpose, usually to do with recreation.
Robert E. Park	Robert E. Park was an American urban sociologist, one of the main founders of the original Chicago School of sociology. He was influential in developing the theory of assimilation as it pertained to immigrants in the United States.
Concept	As the term is used in mainstream cognitive science and philosophy of mind, a concept is an abstract idea or a mental symbol, typically associated with a corresponding representation in and language or symbology.
Consciousness	Consciousness involves thoughts, sensations, perceptions, moods, emotions, dreams, and an awareness of self, although not necessarily any particular one or combination of these. Consciousness is a point of view, an I, or what Thomas Nagel called the existence of "something that it is like" to be something. Julian Jaynes has emphasized that "Consciousness is not the same as cognition and should be sharply distinguished from it. ... The most common error ... is to confuse consciousness with perception." He says, "Mind-space I regard as the primary feature of consciousness. It is the space which you preoptively are 'introspecting on' or 'seeing' at this very moment".
Ethnic identity	Ethnic identity refers to an enduring, basic aspect of the self that includes a sense of membership in an ethnic group and the attitudes and feelings related to that membership. Ethnic identity can vary with changes in social context.
Identity	Identity is an umbrella term used throughout the social sciences to describe an individual's comprehension of him or herself as a discrete, separate entity.
Marginalization	Marginalization refers to the overt or covert trends within societies whereby those perceived as lacking desirable traits or deviating from the group norms tend to be excluded by wider society and ostracised as undesirables.
Washington	Washington is a state in the Pacific Northwest region of the United States. Named after George Washington, it is the only U.S. state named after a president.
Booker T. Washington	Booker T. Washington was an American educator, author and leader of the African American community. He was freed from slavery as a child, gained an education, and as a young man was appointed to lead a teachers' college for blacks. From this position of leadership he rose into a nationally prominent role as spokesman for African Americans.

Merton	Merton coined the phrase "self-fulfilling prophecy." He also coined many other phrases that have gone into everyday use, such as "role model" and "unintended consequences".
City	A city is an urban area with a large population and a particular administrative, legal, or historical status.
Ethnocentrism	Ethnocentrism is the tendency to look at the world primarily from the perspective of one's own culture. It often entails the belief that one's own race or ethnic group is the most important and/or that some or all aspects of its culture are superior to those of other
Grand Theft	Grand theft is a felony crime in the United States defined as the theft of objects exceeding a certain monetary value.
Motor vehicle theft	Motor vehicle theft is the criminal act of stealing or attempting to steal a motor vehicle, including an automobile, truck, bus, motorcycle, snowmobile, trailer or any other motorized vehicle.
Theft	In the criminal law, theft is the illegal taking of another person's property without that person's freely-given consent. As a term, it is used as shorthand for all major crimes against property, encompassing offences such as burglary, embezzlement, larceny, looting, robbery, mugging, trespassing, shoplifting, intrusion, fraud and sometimes criminal conversion.
Vice	Vice is a practice or habit that is considered immoral, depraved, and/or degrading in the associated society.
Crime	A normative definition views crime as deviant behavior that violates prevailing norms, specifically, cultural standards prescribing how humans ought to behave.
Hatred	Hatred is an emotion of intense revulsion, distaste, enmity, or antipathy for a person, thing, or phenomenon, generally attributed to a desire to avoid, restrict, remove, or destroy the hated object. Hatred can be based on fear of an object or past negative consequences of dealing with that object.
Hate crimes	Hate crimes occur when a perpetrator targets a victim because of his or her membership in a certain social group, usually defined by race, religion, sexual orientation, disability, ethnicity, nationality, age, gender, gender identity, or political affiliation. Hate crimes differ from conventional crime because they are not directed simply at an individual, but are meant to cause fear and intimidation in an entire group or class of people.
Prejudice	Prejudice is, as the name implies, the process of "pre-judging" something. It implies coming to a judgment on a subject before learning where the preponderance of evidence actually lies, or forming a judgment without direct experience.
Prevalence	In epidemiology, the prevalence of a disease in a statistical population is defined as the total number of cases of the disease in the population at a given time, or the total number of cases in the population, divided by the number of individuals in the population.
Video game	A video game is a game that involves interaction with a user interface to generate visual feedback on a video device.
Anti-Defamation League	The Anti-Defamation League is an advocacy group founded in 1913 by B'nai B'rith in the United States whose stated aim is "to stop, by appeals to reason and conscience and, if necessary, by appeals to law, the defamation of the Jewish people. Its ultimate purpose is to secure justice and fair treatment to all citizens alike and to put an end forever to unjust and unfair discrimination against and ridicule of any sect or body of citizens."
Crime Statistics	Crime statistics attempt to provide a statistical measure of the level, or amount, of crime that is prevalent in societies. Given that crime, by definition, is an illegal activity, every way of measuring it is likely to be inaccurate. Crime statistics are gathered and

reported by many countries and are of interest to several international organisations, including Interpol and the United Nations.

Gay

Gay usually describes a person's sexual orientation, being the standard term for homosexual. Gay sometimes also refers to commonalities shared by homosexual people, as in "gay history", the ideological concept of a hypothetical gay culture, as in "gay music." The word gay is sometimes used to refer to same-sex relationships.

Hate Crime Statistics Act

The Hate Crime Statistics Act requires the Attorney General to collect data on crimes committed because of the victim's race, religion, disability, sexual orientation, or ethnicity. It is the first federal statute to "recognize and name gay, lesbian and bisexual people."

Lesbian

A lesbian is a woman who is romantically and sexually attracted only to other women. Some women in same-sex relationships do not identify as lesbian, but as bisexual, queer, or another label. As with any interpersonal activity, sexual expression depends on the context of the relationship.

National Gay and Lesbian Task Force

The National Gay and Lesbian Task Force is an organization working for the civil rights of lesbian, gay, bisexual and transgender people in the United States.

Poverty

Poverty may be seen as the collective condition of poor people, or of poor groups, and in this sense entire nation-states are sometimes regarded as poor. Although the most severe poverty is in the developing world, there is evidence of poverty in every region.

Sexual orientation

Sexual orientation describes the direction of an individual's sexuality, often in relation to their own sex or gender. Common terms for describing sexual orientation include bisexual (bi), heterosexual (straight) and homosexual (lesbian/gay).

Southern Poverty Law Center

The Southern Poverty Law Center is an American non-profit legal organization, internationally known for its tolerance education programs, its legal victories against white supremacists and its tracking of hate groups.

Statistics

Statistics is a mathematical science pertaining to the collection, analysis, interpretation, and presentation of data. It is applicable to a wide variety of academic disciplines, from the physical and social sciences to the humanities; it is also used and misused for making informed decisions in all areas of business and government.

Violence

Violence is, on the one hand, acts of aggression and abuse that cause' or intend to cause injury to person or persons. Central to this concept of violence is the presence of the definite intention to cause significant injury, damage and harm.

Groups

In sociology, a group can be defined as two or more humans that interact with one another, accept expectations and obligations as members of the group, and share a common identity. By this definition, society can be viewed as a large group, though most social groups are considerably smaller.

Discrimination

Discrimination refers to the denial of equal access to social resources to people on the basis of their group membership.

Typology

Typology refers to the classification of observations in terms of their attributes on two or more variables. The classification of newspapers as liberal-urban, liberal-rural, conservative-urban, or conservative-rural would be an example of a typology.

Attitude

Attitude is a hypothetical construct that represents an individual's like or dislike for an item. Attitudes are positive, negative or neutral views of an "attitude object": i.e. a person, behavior or event. People can also be "ambivalent" towards a target, meaning that they simultaneously possess a positive and a negative bias towards the attitude in question.

Go to **Cram101.com** for the Practice Tests for this Chapter.

Scapegoating	Blaming, punishing, or stigmatizing a relatively powerless individual or group for wrongs that were not of their doing, is referred to as scapegoating.
Genocide	Genocide is the deliberate and systematic destruction of an ethnic, religious or national group. It is define as "any of the following acts committed with intent to destroy, in whole or in part, a national, ethnical, racial or religious group, as such: killing members of the group; causing serious bodily or mental harm to members of the group; deliberately inflicting on the group conditions of life, calculated to bring about its physical destruction in whole or in part; imposing measures intended to prevent births within the group; forcibly transferring children of the group to another group."
Adorno	Adorno was to a great extent influenced by Walter Benjamin's application of Karl Marx's thought. Adorno, along with other major Frankfurt School theorists such as Horkheimer and Marcuse, argued that advanced capitalism was able to contain or liquidate the forces that would bring about its collapse and that the revolutionary moment, when it would have been possible to transform it into socialism, had passed. Adorno argued that capitalism had become more entrenched through its attack on the objective basis of revolutionary consciousness and through liquidation of the individualism that had been the basis of critical consciousness.
Authoritarianism	Authoritarianism describes a form of government characterized by strict obedience to the authority of the state, which often maintains and enforces social control through the use of oppressive measures. The term may also be used to describe the personality or management style of an individual or organization which seeks to dominate those within its sphere of influence and has little regard for building consensus.
Authoritarian personality	A set of distinctive personality traits, including conformity, intolerance, and an inability to accept ambiguity, is referred to as an authoritarian personality.
Personality	In psychology, personality is a description of consistent emotional, thought, and behavior patterns in a person. The several theoretical perspectives on personality involve different ideas about the relationship between personality and other psychological constructs as well as different ideas about the way personality doesn't develop.
Oliver C. Cox	Oliver C. Cox was a Trinidadian-American sociologist noted for his early Marxist viewpoint on Fascism. He is a member of the Chicago school of sociology. He was Marxist that criticized capitalism and race in Foundations of Capitalism.
Exploitation	In political economy, economics, and sociology, exploitation involves a persistent social relationship in which certain persons are being mistreated or unfairly used for the benefit of others. This corresponds to one ethical conception of exploitation, that is, the treatment of human beings as mere means to an end — or as mere "objects".
Marx	Marx was a 19th century philosopher, political economist, and revolutionary. Marx addressed a wide range of political as well as social issues ; he is most famous for his analysis of history, summed up in the opening line of the Communist Manifesto: "The history of all hitherto existing society is the history of class struggles". Marx believed that capitalism would be displaced by radical socialism which in turn would develop into a communism.
Karl Marx	Karl Marx was a philosopher, political economist, and revolutionary. Marx addressed a wide range of issues; he is most famous for his analysis of history, summed up in the opening line of the Communist Manifesto. Marx believed that the capitalism would be displaced by radical socialism which in turn would develop into a communism - a classless society.
Gordon W. Allport	Gordon W. Allport was an American psychologist. He rejected both a psychoanalytic approach to personality, which he thought often went too deep, and a behavioral approach, which he thought often did not go deep enough. He was one of the first researchers to draw a distinction between Motive and Drive. He suggested that a drive formed as a reaction to a motive may out-grow the motive as a reason.

Normative	In social sciences the term normative is used to describe the effects of those structures of culture which regulate the function of social activity. Those structures thus act to encourage or enforce social activity and outcomes that ought to occur, while discouraging or preventing social activity that ought not occur.
Stereotype	A stereotype is a simplified and/or standardized conception or image with specific meaning, often held in common by one group of people about another group. A stereotype can be a conventional and oversimplified conception, opinion, or image, based on the assumption that there are attributes that members of the other group hold in common. Stereotypes may be positive or negative in tone. They are typically generalizations based on minimal or limited knowledge about a group to which the person doing the stereotyping does not belong. Persons may be grouped based on race, ethnicity, religion, sexual orientation, or any number of other categories.
Stereotyping	Stereotyping refers to a process whereby a trait, usually negative, is generalized to all members of a particular group.
Driving While Black	Driving While Black is an American culture phrase that refers to the alleged criminalization of black drivers. The phrase implies that a motorist may be pulled over by a police officer simply because he or she is black, and then questioned, searched, and/or charged with a trivial offense. This concept stems from a long history of racism in the United States, United Kingdom, and other countries.
Racial profiling	Racial profiling is inclusion of race in the profile of a persons considered likely to commit a particular crime or type of crime.
Ethnicity	Ethnicity is a population of human beings whose members identify with each other, either on the basis of a presumed common genealogy or ancestry or recognition by others as a distinct group, or by common cultural, linguistic, religious, or physical traits. The sociologist Max Weber once remarked that "The whole conception of it is so complex and so vague that it might be good to abandon it altogether."
Guideline	A guideline is any document that aims to streamline particular processes according to a set routine.
Race	The term race refers to the concept of dividing people into populations or groups on the basis of various sets of characteristics and beliefs about common ancestry. The most widely used human racial categories are based on visible traits especially skin color, facial features and hair texture, and self-identification.
Emory Bogardus	Emory Bogardus was a prominent figure in the history of American sociology. He founded one of the first sociology departments at an American university, at the University of Southern California. He also founded Alpha Kappa Delta, the international sociology honor society.
Burgess	Burgess is an English word that originally meant a freeman of a borough or burgh.
Ernest Burgess	Ernest Burgess was an urban sociologist. His groundbreaking social ecology research, in conjunction with his colleague, Robert E. Park, provided the foundation for The Chicago School. In The City, they conceptualized the city into the concentric zones, including the central business district, transitional, working class residential, residential, and commuter/suburban zones.
Hispanic	Hispanic is a term that historically denoted relation to the ancient Hispania and its peoples. The term now refers to the culture and people of the Spanish-speaking countries of Hispanic America and Spain; or countries with a historical legacy from Spain, including the Southwestern United States and Florida; the African nations of Equatorial Guinea, Western Sahara and the Northern coastal region of Morocco; the Asia-Pacific nations of the Philippines, Guam, Northern Mariana Islands; and to the ethnic individuals of those cultures.

	It can also refer to the Hispanosphere geographical distribution, the same way Latin refers to the Romance languages in general.
Hispanic American	Hispanic American is an American citizen or resident of Hispanic ethnicity and can identify themselves as having Hispanic Cultural heritage. According to the 2000 Census, Hispanics constitute the second largest ethnic group in the United States, compromizing roughly 12.5% of the population.
Eric Lichtblau	Eric Lichtblau is an American journalist and Washington bureau reporter for The New York Times. He did stints on the L.A. Times investigative team in Los Angeles and covered various law enforcement beats. He is the author of Bush's Law: The Remaking of American Justice.
Park	A park is a bounded area of land, usually in its natural or semi-natural landscaped state and set aside for some purpose, usually to do with recreation.
Robert E. Park	Robert E. Park was an American urban sociologist, one of the main founders of the original Chicago School of sociology. He was influential in developing the theory of assimilation as it pertained to immigrants in the United States.
Social distance	Social distance describes the distance between different groups of society and is opposed to locational distance. The notion includes all differences such as social class, race/ethnicity or sexuality, but also the fact that the different groups do not mix. The term is often applied in cities, but its use is not limited to that.
Lawrence Bobo	Lawrence Bobo is the Martin Luther King Jr. Centennial Professor at Standford University. He is also the Director of the Center for Comparative Studies in Race and Ethnicity. He has made central contributions to both the understanding of racial attitudes and relations in the United States. He is co-author of Racial Attitudes in America: Trends and Interpretations.
Tom W. Smith	Tom W. Smith is Director of the General Social Survey of the National Opinion Research Center. His areas of expertise are surveys: methodology, social, change, and international. He is an internationally recognized expert in survey research specializing in the study of societal change and survey methodology.
Integration	Social integration is a term used in sociology and several other social sciences. The term indicates different meanings depending on the context. In general, it connotes the process of combining a group of persons like minority groups, ethnic minorities, refugees, underprivileged sections of the society, to integrate into the mainstream of the society, and thus to avail of the opportunities, rights and services available to the members of the mainstream of the society. It is important to note that within the field of sociology social integration usually goes hand in hand with social solidarity and anomie.
Racism	Racism, by its simplest definition, is discrimination based on race. People with racist beliefs might hate certain groups of people according to their race, or in the case of institutional racism, certain racial groups may be denied rights or benefits. Racism typically starts with the assumption that there are taxonomic differences between different groups of people. According to the United Nations conventions, there is no distinction between the term racial discrimination and ethnic discrimination.
Brown v. Board of Education	Brown v. Board of Education was a landmark decision of the United States Supreme Court, which overturned earlier rulings going back to Plessy v. Ferguson in 1896, by declaring that state laws which established separate public schools for black and white students denied black children equal educational opportunities.
Kenneth McKenzie Clark	Kenneth McKenzie Clark was an English author, museum director, broadcaster, and one of the most famous art historians of his generation. In 1969, he was catapulted to international fame as the writer, producer and presenter of the BBC Television series, Civilisation: A Personal View.

Go to **Cram101.com** for the Practice Tests for this Chapter.

Oppression	Oppression is the negative outcome experienced by people targeted by the cruel exercise of power in a society or social group. It is particularly closely associated with nationalism and derived social systems, wherein identity is built by antagonism to the other.
Self-esteem	In psychology, self-esteem reflects a person's overall self-appraisal of his or her own worth.
Status	In sociology or anthropology, social status is the honor or prestige attached to one's position in society one's social position. The stratification system, which is the system of distributing rewards to the members of society, determines social status. Social status, the position or rank of a person or group within the stratification system, can be determined two ways. One can earn their social status by their own achievements, which is known as achieved status, or one can be placed in the stratification system by their inherited position, which is called ascribed status.
Hostility	Hostility is a form of angry internal rejection or denial in psychology.
Mass media	Mass media refers to forms of communication designed to reach a vast audience without any personal contact between the senders and receivers.
Media	In communication, media are the storage and transmission tools used to store and deliver information or data. It is often referred to as synonymous with mass media or news media, but may refer to a single medium used to communicate any data for any purpose.
Separate but equal	Separate but equal is a phrase used to describe a system of segregation, where people of different ethnic backgrounds (or, in practice, people simply perceived to be different from each other in a manner considered significant enough to justify segregationist policies or practices) have the same qualitative and quantitative rights to services and facilities, but receive them apart from each other.
Boycott	A boycott is the act of voluntarily abstaining from using, buying, or dealing with someone or some other organization as an expression of protest.
Dominance	In animal colonies, a condition established by one animal over another by prevailing in an aggressive encounter between the two, is referred to as dominance.
Television	Television is a widely used telecommunication medium for sending and receiving moving monochromatic or color images, usually accompanied by sound. "Television" may also refer specifically to a television set, television programming or television transmission. The word is derived from mixed Latin and Greek roots, meaning "far sight": Greek tele, far, and Latin vision, sight.
African Americans	African Americans are citizens or residents of the United States whose ancestors, usually in predominant part, were indigenous to Sub-Saharan Africa. Most are the descendants of captive Africans who were enslaved within the boundaries of the present United States.
Contact	In Family Law, contact is one of the general terms which denotes the level of contact a parent or other significant person in a child's life can have with that child. Contact forms part of the bundle of rights and privileges which a parent may have in relation to any child of the family.
Contact hypothesis	The notion that prejudice can be reduced through increased contact among members of different social groups is referred to as contact hypothesis.
Entertainment	Entertainment is an activity designed to give people pleasure or relaxation.
Hypothesis	A hypothesis consists either of a suggested explanation for a phenomenon or of a reasoned proposal suggesting a possible correlation between multiple phenomena. The term derives from the Greek, hypotithenai meaning "to put under" or "to suppose." The scientific method requires that one can test a scientific hypothesis. Scientists generally base such hypotheses

on previous observations or on extensions of scientific theories. Even though the words "hypothesis" and "theory" are often used synonymously in common and informal usage, a scientific hypothesis is not the same as a scientific theory.

Cultural diversity

Cultural diversity is the variety of human societies or cultures in a specific region, or in the world as a whole.

Workplace

A workplace is any plant, yard, premises, room or other vicinity where employees engage in the performance of labor or service over which an employer has the right of access and control.

Training

The term training refers to the acquisition of knowledge, skills, and competencies as a result of the teaching of vocational or practical skills and knowledge that relate to specific useful competencies.

Sendhil Mullainathan

Sendhil Mullainathan is a Professor of Economics at Harvard University. He was hired with tenure by Harvard in 2004 after having spent six years at MIT, first as a junior faculty member and then as a full Professor. He is a recipient of a MacArthur Foundation "genius grant" and conducts research on development economics, behavioral economics, and corporate finance. He is currently a Director of the Financial Access Initiative. Mullainathan received his B.A. in Computer Science, Mathematics, and Economics from Cornell University in 1993 and his Ph.D. in Economics from Harvard in 1998. Although he was born in a small farming village in India, Mullainathan moved to the Los Angeles area at age seven.

Interview

An interview is a conversation between two or more people where questions are asked by the interviewer to obtain information from the interviewee. The most common type of interview for assessment is a job interview between an employer and an applicant. The goal of such an interview is to assess a potential employee to see if he/she has the social skills and intelligence suitable for the workplace.

John F. Kennedy

John F. Kennedy was the thirty-fifth President of the United States, serving from 1961 until his assassination in 1963.

Relative deprivation	Relative deprivation is the experience of being deprived of something to which one thinks one is entitled. Schaefer defines it as "the conscious experience of a negative discrepancy between legitimate expectations and present actualities." It is a term used in social
Absolute deprivation	A lack of basic necessities relative to a fixed standard such as the amount of food necessary for survival is referred to as absolute deprivation.
Marx	Marx was a 19th century philosopher, political economist, and revolutionary. Marx addressed a wide range of political as well as social issues ; he is most famous for his analysis of history, summed up in the opening line of the Communist Manifesto: "The history of all hitherto existing society is the history of class struggles". Marx believed that capitalism would be displaced by radical socialism which in turn would develop into a communism.
Karl Marx	Karl Marx was a philosopher, political economist, and revolutionary. Marx addressed a wide range of issues; he is most famous for his analysis of history, summed up in the opening line of the Communist Manifesto. Marx believed that the capitalism would be displaced by radical socialism which in turn would develop into a communism - a classless society.
Discrimination	Discrimination refers to the denial of equal access to social resources to people on the basis of their group membership.
Workplace	A workplace is any plant, yard, premises, room or other vicinity where employees engage in the performance of labor or service over which an employer has the right of access and control.
Stokely Carmichael	Stokely Carmichael was a Trinidadian-American black activist active in the 1960s American Civil Rights Movement. He rose to prominence first as a leader of the Student Nonviolent Coordinating Committee and later as the "Honorary Prime Minister" of the Black Panther Party.
Institution	Institution refers to structures and mechanisms of social order and cooperation governing the behavior of two or more individuals. They are identified with a social purpose and permanence, transcending individual human lives and intentions, and with the making and enforcing of rules governing cooperative human behavior.
Institutional discrimination	Accepted social arrangements that place minority groups at a disadvantage are referred to as institutional discrimination.
Informal economy	In economics, the term informal economy refers to the general market income category (or sector) wherein certain types of income and the means of their generation are "unregulated by the institutions of society, in a legal and social environment in which similar activities are regulated."
Security	Security is the condition of being protected against danger or loss.
Underground economy	The underground economy consists of all commerce on which applicable taxes are being evaded. The market includes not only legally-prohibited commerce, but also trade in legal goods and services because some income is not reported and consequently taxation is evaded, e.g., through money laundering, payment in cash, or other means.
Economy	An economy is the system of human activities related to the production, distribution, exchange, and consumption of goods and services of a country or other area. The composition of a given economy is inseparable from technological evolution, civilization's history and social organization.
Labor	In economics, labor is a measure of the work done by human beings. It is conventionally contrasted with such other factors of production as land and capital. There are theories which have created a concept called human capital, although there are also counter posing macro-economic system theories that think human capital is a contradiction in terms.
Edna Bonacich	Edna Bonacich is Professor of Sociology and Ethnic Studies at the University of California,

Go to **Cram101.com** for the Practice Tests for this Chapter.
And, **NEVER** highlight a book again!

Riverside. Her major research interest has been the study of class and race, with emphasis on racial divisions in the working class. One of her books is The Garment Industry in the Restructuring Global Economy.

Student	A student could be described as 'one who directs zeal at a subject'.
Sweatshop	Sweatshop is a pejorative term used to describe a manufacturing facility, usually a garment manufacturing facility, where working conditions are poor and workers are paid little. It has proved a difficult issue to resolve because their roots lie in the conceptual foundations of the world economy.
Market	A market is a social arrangement that allows buyers and sellers to discover information and carry out a voluntary exchange of goods or services. It is one of the two key institutions that organize trade, along with the right to own property.
William Julius Wilson	William Julius Wilson is an American sociologist. In The Declining Significance of Race: Blacks and Changing American Institutions he argues that the significance of race is waning, and an African-American's class is comparatively more important in determining his or her life chances.
Legal services	Most liberal democracies consider it necessary to provide some level of legal services to persons otherwise unable to afford legal representation. To fail to do so would deprive such persons of access to the court system. Alternately, they would be at a disadvantage in situations in which the state or a wealthy individual took them to court. This would violate the principles of equality before the law and due process under the rule of law.
Median	The number that falls halfway in a range of numbers, or the score below which are half the scores and above which are the other half is a median.
Median household income	The median household income is commonly used to provide data about geographic areas and divides households into two equal segments with the first half of households earning less than the median household income and the other half earning more. The median household income is considered by many statisticians to be a better indicator than the average household income as it is not dramatically affected by unusually high or low values.
Ethnicity	Ethnicity is a population of human beings whose members identify with each other, either on the basis of a presumed common genealogy or ancestry or recognition by others as a distinct group, or by common cultural, linguistic, religious, or physical traits. The sociologist Max Weber once remarked that "The whole conception of it is so complex and so vague that it might be good to abandon it altogether."
Gender	Gender refers to the differences between men and women. Gender identity is an individual's self-conception as being male or female, as distinguished from actual biological sex. In general, gender often refers to purely social rather than biological differences.
Income	Income, generally defined, is the money that is received as a result of the normal business activities of an individual or a business.
Race	The term race refers to the concept of dividing people into populations or groups on the basis of various sets of characteristics and beliefs about common ancestry. The most widely used human racial categories are based on visible traits especially skin color, facial features and hair texture, and self-identification.
Gross domestic product	A region's gross domestic product of a country is defined as the market value of all final goods and services produced within a country in a given period of time. It is also considered the sum of value added at every stage of production of all final goods and services produced within a country in a given period of time.
Voluntary	A voluntary association is a group of individuals who voluntarily enter into an agreement to

Go to **Cram101.com** for the Practice Tests for this Chapter.

association	form a body (or organization) to accomplish a purpose.
Brown v. Board of Education	Brown v. Board of Education was a landmark decision of the United States Supreme Court, which overturned earlier rulings going back to Plessy v. Ferguson in 1896, by declaring that state laws which established separate public schools for black and white students denied black children equal educational opportunities.
Civil Rights	Civil rights are the protections and privileges of personal liberty given to all citizens by law. Civil rights are rights that are bestowed by nations on those within their territorial boundaries.
Dred Scott v. Sandford	Dred Scott v. Sandford, 60 U.S. 393, was a lawsuit, pivotal in the history of the United States, decided by the United States Supreme Court in 1857 that ruled that people of African descent, whether or not they were slaves, could never be citizens of the United States, and that Congress had no authority to prohibit slavery in federal territories.
Equal Employment Opportunity Commission	The Equal Employment Opportunity Commission is a United States federal agency tasked with ending employment discrimination in the United States. It also serves as an adjudicatory for claims of discrimination brought against federal agencies.
Judicial branch	Judicial branch is the system of courts which administer justice in the name of the sovereign or state, a mechanism for the resolution of disputes. The term is also used to refer collectively to the judges, magistrates and other adjudicators who form the core of it, as well as the support personnel who keep the system running smoothly.
Legislation	Legislation is law which has been promulgated by a legislature or other governing body. The term may refer to a single law, or the collective body of enacted law, while "statute" is also used to refer to a single law. Before an item of legislation becomes law it may be known as a bill, which is typically also known as "legislation" while it remains under active consideration.
City	A city is an urban area with a large population and a particular administrative, legal, or historical status.
New York	New York is a state in the Mid-Atlantic and Northeastern regions of the United States of America. With 62 counties, it is the country's third most populous state. It is bordered by Vermont, Massachusetts, Connecticut, New Jersey, and Pennsylvania, and shares a water border with Rhode Island as well as an international border with the Canadian provinces of Quebec and Ontario. Its five largest cities are New York City, Buffalo, Rochester, Yonkers, and Syracuse.
Redlining	Redlining is the practice of denying or increasing the cost of services, such as banking, insurance, access to jobs, access to health care, or even supermarkets to residents in certain, often racially determined, areas. The most devastating form of redlining, and the most common use of the term, refers to mortgage discrimination, in which middle-income black and Hispanic residents are denied loans that are made available to lower-income whites.
Taylor	Taylor was an American engineer who sought to improve industrial efficiency. He was one of the intellectual leaders of the Efficiency Movement and his ideas, broadly conceived, were highly influential in the Progressive Era. During the latter part of his career he was a management consultant, and he is sometimes called "The Father of Scientific Management."
Tiger Woods	Tiger Woods whose achievements to date rank him among the most successful golfers of all time. Currently the World No. 1, Woods was the highest-paid professional athlete in 2007, having earned an estimated $122 million from winnings and endorsements. According to Golf Digest, Woods made $769,440,709 from 1996 to 2007, and the magazine predicts that by 2010, Woods will become the world's first athlete to pass one billion dollars in earnings.

Go to **Cram101.com** for the Practice Tests for this Chapter.

Social impact	In business and government policy, social impact refers to how the organization's actions affect the surrounding community.
Environmental movement	The environmental movement is a diverse scientific, social, and political movement. In general terms, environmentalists advocate the sustainable management of resources and stewardship of the natural environment through changes in public policy and individual behavior.
Environmental Protection Agency	The Environmental Protection Agency is an agency of the federal government of the United States charged with protecting human health and with safeguarding the natural environment: air, water, and land.
Environmental justice	Environmental justice is a term in the social sciences used to describe injustices in the way natural resources are used. Environmental justice is a holistic effort to analyze and overcome the power structures that have traditionally thwarted environmental reforms.
Pollution	Pollution is the introduction of pollutants into the environment which result in deleterious effects of such a nature as to endanger human health, harm living resources and ecosystems, and impair or interfere with amenities and other legitimate uses of the environment.
Environmental racism	Environmental racism is intentional or unintentional racial discrimination in the enforcement of environmental rules and regulations, the intentional or unintentional targeting of minority communities for the siting of polluting industries such as toxic waste disposal, or the exclusion of people of color from public and private boards, commissions, and regulatory bodies.
Justice	Justice concerns the proper ordering of things and persons within a society. As a concept it has been subject to philosophical, legal, and theological reflection and debate throughout history.
Racism	Racism, by its simplest definition, is discrimination based on race. People with racist beliefs might hate certain groups of people according to their race, or in the case of institutional racism, certain racial groups may be denied rights or benefits. Racism typically starts with the assumption that there are taxonomic differences between different groups of people. According to the United Nations conventions, there is no distinction between the term racial discrimination and ethnic discrimination.
Affirmative action	Affirmative action refers to policies intended to promote access to education or employment aimed at a historically socio-politically non-dominant group. Motivation for affirmative action policies is to redress the effects of past discrimination and to encourage public institutions such as universities, hospitals and police forces to be more representative of the population.
Sex	Sex refers to the male and female duality of biology and reproduction. Unlike organisms that only have the ability to reproduce asexually, male and female pairs have the ability to produce offspring through meiosis and fertilization.
Minority	A minority is a sociological group that does not constitute a politically dominant plurality of the total population of a given society. A sociological minority is not necessarily a numerical minority it may include any group that is disadvantaged with respect to a dominant group in terms of social status, education, employment, wealth and political power.
Government	A government is a body that has the authority to make and the power to enforce laws within a civil, corporate, religious, academic, or other organization or group.
Higher education	Higher education is education provided by universities, vocational universities and other collegial institutions that award academic degrees, such as career colleges. Higher education includes teaching, research and social services activities of universities, and within the realm of teaching, it includes both the undergraduate level and the graduate level.

Go to **Cram101.com** for the Practice Tests for this Chapter.

Linda Greenhouse	Linda Greenhouse a Pulitzer Prize winning reporter who covered the United States Supreme Court for three decades for the The New York Times. She has also faced criticism for expressing publicly, her personal views supporting abortion rights and criticism of US policies and actions at Guantanamo Bay, Abu Ghraib, and Haditha.
Reverse discrimination	Reverse discrimination includes discriminatory policies or acts that benefit a historically socio-politically non-dominant group (typically women and minorities), at the expense of a historically socio-politically dominant group (typically men and majority races). Reverse discrimination is itself a form of discrimination.
Howard Winant	Howard Winant is an American sociologist and race theorist. Professor Winant is most well known for developing the theory of racial formation along with Michael Omi. Currently, Winant is Professor of Sociology at the University of California, Santa Barbara. Winant's research and teachings revolve around race and racism, comparative historical sociology, political sociology, social theory, and human rights.
Glass ceiling	Glass ceiling refers to barriers based on attitudinal or organizational bias that prevent qualified females from advancing to top-level positions.
Glass escalator	The term glass elevator or glass escalator is used to describe the rapid promotion of men over women, especially into management, in female-dominated fields like nursing.
Strauss	Strauss was an American sociologist, who worked the field of medical sociology. Strauss is best known for his work on the methodology in qualitative research and in particular for the development of grounded theory, a general methodology he established together with Barney Glaser in the 1960s.
Max weber	Max Weber was a German political economist and sociologist who is considered one of the founders of the modern study of sociology and public administration. His major works deal with rationalisation in sociology of religion and government, but he also contributed much in the field of economics. His most famous work is his essay The Protestant Ethic and the Spirit of Capitalism, which began his work in the sociology of religion.
Derrick Bell	Derrick Bell is a visiting professor of Constitutional Law at New York University School of Law for the past years and a major figure within the legal studies discipline of Critical Race Theory.
Future	The future is commonly understood to contain all events that have yet to occur. It is the opposite of the past, and is the time after the present. Organized efforts to predict or forecast the future may have derived from observations by early man of heavenly objects. In physics, which uses a linear conception of time, the future is the portion of the projected time line that is anticipated to occur. In special relativity the future is considered as absolute future or the future light cone. In physics, time is considered to be a fourth dimension

Citizenship	Citizenship is membership in a society, community, or and carries with it rights to political participation; a person having such membership is a citizen.
Status	In sociology or anthropology, social status is the honor or prestige attached to one's position in society one's social position. The stratification system, which is the system of distributing rewards to the members of society, determines social status. Social status,
Voting	Voting is a method of decision making wherein a group such as a meeting or an electorate attempts to gauge its opinion—usually as a final step following discussions or debates.
Population	A population is the collection of people or organisms of a particular species living in a given geographic area or space, usually measured by a census.
Social forces	Social forces are the typical basic drives, or motives, which lead to the fundamental types of association and group relationship.
Immigration	Although human migration has existed for hundreds of thousands of years, immigration in the modern sense refers to movement of people from one nation-state to another, where they are not citizens.
Catholicism	Catholicism is a denomination of Christianity whose center is the Vatican in Rome, Italy and dates from the original church created by the Apostle Peter, a disciple of Jesus Christ.
Chinese Exclusion Act	The Chinese Exclusion Act was a United States federal law passed on May 6, 1882, following 1880 revisions to the Burlingame Treaty of 1868. Those revisions allowed the U.S. to suspend immigration, and Congress subsequently acted quickly to implement the suspension of Chinese immigration.
Chinese immigration to the United States	Chinese immigration to the United States mainly consists of three major waves with the first beginning in the early 19th century. For nearly two centuries, the history of Chinese immigration to the United States has witnessed hardship as well as success.
Conspiracy	In the criminal law, a conspiracy is an agreement between natural persons to break the law at some time in the future, and, in some cases, with at least one overt act in furtherance of that agreement. There is no limit on the number participating in the conspiracy and, in most countries, no requirement that any steps have been taken to put the plan into effect compare attempts which require proximity to the full offence.
John B. Duff	John B. Duff is an American historian. His publications include The Structure of American History, The Nat Turner Rebellion: The Historical Event Controversy, The Irish in the United States, and Slavery: Its Origins and Legacy. He was president of Columbia College Chicago and oversaw the acquisition of the college's first residence hall, led its first long-range planning effort and expanded its local and national development initiatives.
Know Nothing movement	The Know Nothing movement was a nativist American political movement of the 1850s. It was empowered by popular fears that the country was being overwhelmed by Irish Catholic immigrants, who were often regarded as hostile to US values and controlled by the Pope in Rome. Mainly active from 1854–56, it strove to curb immigration and naturalization, though its efforts met with little success.
Ku Klux Klan	Ku Klux Klan is the name of several past and present organizations in the United States that have advocated white supremacy, antisemitism, racism, homophobia, and nativism. These organizations have often used terrorism, violence and acts of intimidation, such as cross lighting to oppress African Americans, and other social or ethnic groups.
Nativism	Although opposition to immigration is a feature of all countries with immigration, the term nativism originated in American politics and has a specific meaning. Strictly speaking, the term nativism distinguishes between Americans who were born in the United States, and

individuals who have immigrated - 'first generation' immigrants.

Sam Bass Warner	Sam Bass Warner is a Visiting Professor of Urban Studies and Planning at the Massachussetts Instiute of Technology. He is the author of The Way We Really Live: Social Change in Metropolitan Boston Since 1920 and of The Urban Wilderness: A History of the American City.
Xenophobia	Xenophobia is a fear or contempt of foreigners or strangers. The term is typically used to describe fear or dislike of foreigners or in general of people different from one's self.
Violence	Violence is, on the one hand, acts of aggression and abuse that cause' or intend to cause injury to person or persons. Central to this concept of violence is the presence of the definite intention to cause significant injury, damage and harm.
Labor	In economics, labor is a measure of the work done by human beings. It is conventionally contrasted with such other factors of production as land and capital. There are theories which have created a concept called human capital, although there are also counter posing macro-economic system theories that think human capital is a contradiction in terms.
American Federation of Labor	The American Federation of Labor was one of the first federations of labor unions in the United States. It was founded in Columbus, Ohio in 1886 by Samuel Gompers as a reorganization of its predecessor, the Federation of Organized Trades and Labor Unions.
Chinese Americans	Chinese Americans are Americans of Chinese descent. Chinese Americans constitute one group of Overseas Chinese and are a subgroup of Asian Americans.
Emma Lazarus	Emma Lazarus was an American poet born in New York City. She is best known for writing "The New Colossus", a sonnet written in 1883, that was engraved in 1912 on a bronze plaque on a wall in the base of the Statue of Liberty.
Liberty	Liberty is generally considered a concept of political philosophy and identifies the condition in which an individual has the ability to act according to his or her own will.
Race	The term race refers to the concept of dividing people into populations or groups on the basis of various sets of characteristics and beliefs about common ancestry. The most widely used human racial categories are based on visible traits especially skin color, facial features and hair texture, and self-identification.
Statue of Liberty	The statue of liberty is a large statue that was presented to the United States by France. It stands at Liberty Island, New York in New York Harbor as a welcome to all visitors, immigrants, and returning Americans. Worldwide, the Statue of Liberty is one of the most recognizable icons of the United States, and, more generally, represents liberty and escape from oppression.
Ronald Takaki	Ronald Takaki is an ethnic studies historian. His work helps dispel stereotypes of Asian Americans such as the model minority myth. He was inspired to fight for equality for the Asian American community from his personal experiences. Early in his life he faced discrimination as a college student in midwestern America.
Howard Winant	Howard Winant is an American sociologist and race theorist. Professor Winant is most well known for developing the theory of racial formation along with Michael Omi. Currently, Winant is Professor of Sociology at the University of California, Santa Barbara. Winant's research and teachings revolve around race and racism, comparative historical sociology, political sociology, social theory, and human rights.
Denial	Denial is a defense mechanism in which a person is faced with a fact that is too uncomfortable to accept and rejects it instead, insisting that it is not true despite what may be overwhelming evidence.
Organization	In sociology organization is understood as planned, coordinated and purposeful action of human beings to construct or compile a common tangible or intangible product or service.

Literacy	The traditional definition of literacy is considered to be the ability to read and write, or the ability to use language to read, write, listen, and speak. Literacy involves a continuum of learning to enable an individual to achieve his or her goals, to develop his or her knowledge and potential, and to participate fully in the wider society."
Woodrow Wilson	Thomas Woodrow Wilson, was the twenty-eighth President of the United States. A devout Presbyterian and leading "intellectual" of the Progressive Era, he served as president of Princeton University then became the reform governor of New Jersey in 1910.
Policy	A policy is a deliberate plan of action to guide decisions and achieve rational outcomes. The term may apply to government, private sector organizations and groups, and individuals. Presidential executive orders, corporate privacy policies, and parliamentary rules of order are all examples of policy. Policy differs from rules or law. While law can compel or prohibit behaviors policy merely guides actions toward those that are most likely to achieve a desired outcome.
Lyndon Baines Johnson	Lyndon Baines Johnson was the thirty-sixth President of the United States, serving from 1963-1969. A Democrat, Johnson succeeded to the presidency following the assassination of President Kennedy, and after completing Kennedy's term was elected President in his own right in a landslide victory in the 1964 Presidential election.
Naturalization	The origin of the term naturalization is that it gives to a resident alien almost all of the rights held by a natural-born citizen.
Brain	In animals, the brain is the control center of the central nervous system, responsible for behavior. In mammals, the brain is located in the head, protected by the skull and close to the primary sensory apparatus of vision, hearing, equilibrioception, sense of taste, and olfaction.
Brain drain	Brain drain refers to the persistent loss of the most capable people of a country or region, especially their young people, by emigration due to the lure of opportunities and benefits elsewhere.
Illegal	illegal is used to describe something that is prohibited or not authorized by law or, more generally, by rules specific to a particular situation such as a game.
Population growth	Population growth is change in population over time, and can be quantified as the change in the number of individuals in a population per unit time. The term population growth can technically refer to any species, but almost always refers to humans, and it is often used informally for the more specific demographic term population growth rate , and is often used to refer specifically to the growth of the population of the world.
Statistics	Statistics is a mathematical science pertaining to the collection, analysis, interpretation, and presentation of data. It is applicable to a wide variety of academic disciplines, from the physical and social sciences to the humanities; it is also used and misused for making informed decisions in all areas of business and government.
Reform	A reform movement is a kind of social movement that aims to make gradual change, or change in certain aspects of society rather than rapid or fundamental changes.
Hispanic	Hispanic is a term that historically denoted relation to the ancient Hispania and its peoples. The term now refers to the culture and people of the Spanish-speaking countries of Hispanic America and Spain; or countries with a historical legacy from Spain, including the Southwestern United States and Florida; the African nations of Equatorial Guinea, Western Sahara and the Northern coastal region of Morocco; the Asia-Pacific nations of the Philippines, Guam, Northern Mariana Islands; and to the ethnic individuals of those cultures. It can also refer to the Hispanosphere geographical distribution, the same way Latin refers
La Raza	La Raza is sometimes used to denote people of the Latino and Chicano world, as well by

49

	Mestizos who share the pride of their Native American or national Hispanic heritage. Nonetheless, the term and idea associated with it have been mainly adopted by some Mexican people in the United States to express pride in their nation.
Homeland Security	Homeland security is the term generally used to refer to the broad national effort by all levels of government--federal, state, local and tribal--to protect the territory of the United States from hazards both internal and external, natural and man-made, as well as the Department of Homeland Security itself.
Security	Security is the condition of being protected against danger or loss.
Michael Fix	Michael Fix is Vice President and Director of Studies at Migration Policy Institute. His work explores immigrant integration, citizenship policy, immigrant children and families, the education of immigrant children, the effect of welfare reform on immigrants, and the impact of immigrants on the US labor force. He is also an attorney, who served as a Principal Research Associate at the Urban Institute.
Socioeconomic status	Socioeconomic status is a combined measure of an individual's or family's economic and social position relative to others, based on income, education, and occupation.When analyzing a family's SES, the mother's and father's education and occupation are examined, as well as combined income, versus with an individual, when their own attributes are assessed.
Wayne A. Cornelius	Wayne A. Cornelius is Director of Center for Comparative Immigration Studies at the University of California, San Diego. His projects focuses on a comparative analysis of immigration control measures and their outcomes in eleven industrialized nations. As well, a project on the administration of justice in Mexico. One of his selected publications is The International Migration of the Highly-Skilled.
Jared Diamond	Jared Diamond is an American evolutionary biologist, physiologist, biogeographer, lecturer, and nonfiction author. His best-known work is the non-fiction Guns, Germs, and Steel, which asserts that the main international issues of our time are legacies of processes that began during the early-modern period, in which civilizations that had experienced an extensive amount of "human development" began to intrude upon technologically less advanced civilizations around the world.
Globalization	Globalization refers to increasing global connectivity, integration and interdependence in the economic, social, technological, cultural, political, and ecological spheres. It is a unitary process inclusive of many sub-processes that are increasingly binding people and the biosphere more tightly into one global system.
Taylor	Taylor was an American engineer who sought to improve industrial efficiency. He was one of the intellectual leaders of the Efficiency Movement and his ideas, broadly conceived, were highly influential in the Progressive Era. During the latter part of his career he was a management consultant, and he is sometimes called "The Father of Scientific Management."
Legislation	Legislation is law which has been promulgated by a legislature or other governing body. The term may refer to a single law, or the collective body of enacted law, while "statute" is also used to refer to a single law. Before an item of legislation becomes law it may be known as a bill, which is typically also known as "legislation" while it remains under active consideration.
Refugee	According to the 1951 United Nations Convention Relating to the Status of a Refugee, a refugee is a person who owing to a well-founded fear of being persecuted for reasons of race, religion, nationality, membership of a particular social group, or political opinion, is outside the country of their nationality, and is unable to or, owing to such fear, is unwilling to avail him/herself of the protection of that country.
Transnationalism	Transnationalism is a social movement grown out of the heightened interconnectivity between

Go to **Cram101.com** for the Practice Tests for this Chapter.

	people all around the world and the loosening of boundaries between countries.
American Dilemma	An American Dilemma: The Negro Problem and Modern Democracy is a 1944 study of race relations authored by Swedish economist Gunnar Myrdal and funded by The Carnegie Foundation. The foundation chose Myrdal because it thought that as a non-American, he could offer a more unbiased opinion. Myrdal's volume, at nearly 1,500 pages, painstakingly detailed what he saw as obstacles to full participation in American society that were faced by African-Americans as of the 1940s. It sold over 100,000 copies and went through 25 printings before going into its second edition in 1965. It was enormously influential in how racial issues were viewed in the United States, and it was cited in the landmark Brown v. Board case "in general." The book was generally positive in its outlook on the future of race relations in
Myrdal, Gunnar	Myrdal, Gunnar was a Swedish economist and politician. He, along with Friedrich von Hayek, won the Nobel Prize for Economics for their "pioneering work in the theory of money and economic fluctuations and for their penetrating analysis of the interdependence of economic, social and institutional phenomena." He was also known for his study, An American Dilemma: The Negro Problem and Modern Democracy, which influenced the US Supreme Court decision in Brown v. Board of Education to outlaw racial segregation in public schools.

German Americans	German Americans are citizens of the United States of ethnic German ancestry and currently form the largest self-reported ancestry group in the United States, accounting for 17% of the
Mary Waters	Mary Waters is a socialist journalist and activist in the United States. She became the editor of their youth paper, Young Socialist, and the national secretary of the Young Socialist Alliance. Her along with Jack Barnes and others in the SWP leadership, began to
Cultural diversity	Cultural diversity is the variety of human societies or cultures in a specific region, or in the world as a whole.
Population	A population is the collection of people or organisms of a particular species living in a given geographic area or space, usually measured by a census.
Noel Ignatiev	Noel Ignatiev is an American history professor at the Massachusetts College of Art best known for his call to "abolish" the white race. Ignatiev is the co-founder and co-editor of the journal Race Traitor and the New Abolitionist Society. He also has written a book on antebellum northern racism against Irish immigrants, How the Irish Became White.
Marx	Marx was a 19th century philosopher, political economist, and revolutionary. Marx addressed a wide range of political as well as social issues ; he is most famous for his analysis of history, summed up in the opening line of the Communist Manifesto: "The history of all hitherto existing society is the history of class struggles". Marx believed that capitalism would be displaced by radical socialism which in turn would develop into a communism.
Karl Marx	Karl Marx was a philosopher, political economist, and revolutionary. Marx addressed a wide range of issues; he is most famous for his analysis of history, summed up in the opening line of the Communist Manifesto. Marx believed that the capitalism would be displaced by radical socialism which in turn would develop into a communism - a classless society.
Attitude	Attitude is a hypothetical construct that represents an individual's like or dislike for an item. Attitudes are positive, negative or neutral views of an "attitude object": i.e. a person, behavior or event. People can also be "ambivalent" towards a target, meaning that they simultaneously possess a positive and a negative bias towards the attitude in question.
Concept	As the term is used in mainstream cognitive science and philosophy of mind, a concept is an abstract idea or a mental symbol, typically associated with a corresponding representation in and language or symbology.
Ethnic identity	Ethnic identity refers to an enduring, basic aspect of the self that includes a sense of membership in an ethnic group and the attitudes and feelings related to that membership. Ethnic identity can vary with changes in social context.
Ethnicity	Ethnicity is a population of human beings whose members identify with each other, either on the basis of a presumed common genealogy or ancestry or recognition by others as a distinct group, or by common cultural, linguistic, religious, or physical traits. The sociologist Max Weber once remarked that "The whole conception of it is so complex and so vague that it might be good to abandon it altogether."
Identity	Identity is an umbrella term used throughout the social sciences to describe an individual's comprehension of him or herself as a discrete, separate entity.
Immigration	Although human migration has existed for hundreds of thousands of years, immigration in the modern sense refers to movement of people from one nation-state to another, where they are not citizens.
Race	The term race refers to the concept of dividing people into populations or groups on the basis of various sets of characteristics and beliefs about common ancestry. The most widely used human racial categories are based on visible traits especially skin color, facial features and hair texture, and self-identification.

Social construction	A social construction is an institutionalized entity or artifact in a social system 'invented' or 'constructed' by participants in a particular culture or society that exists solely because people agree to behave as if it exists, or agree to follow certain conventional rules.
Statistics	Statistics is a mathematical science pertaining to the collection, analysis, interpretation, and presentation of data. It is applicable to a wide variety of academic disciplines, from the physical and social sciences to the humanities; it is also used and misused for making informed decisions in all areas of business and government.
Peggy McIntosh	Peggy McIntosh is an American feminist and anti-racist activist, a speaker and the founder and co-director of the National S.E.E.D. Project on Inclusive Curriculum. She is most famous for authoring "White Privilege and Male Privilege: A Personal Account of Coming to See Correspondences through Work in Women's Studies."
Devah Pager	Devah Pager is Professor of Sociology at the Princeton University. Her research focuses on institutions affection racial stratification, including education, labor markets, and criminal justice system. She has research a seried of field experiments studying discrimination agains minorities and ex-offenders in the low-wage labor market.
Privilege	A privilege—etymologically "private law" or law relating to a specific individual—is a special entitlement or immunity granted by a government or other authority to a restricted group, either by birth or on a conditional basis. A privilege can be revoked in some cases. In modern democracies, a privilege is conditional and granted only after birth. By contrast, a right is an inherent, irrevocable entitlement held by all citizens or all human beings from birth. Miscellaneous privileges, e.g. the old common law privilege to title deeds, may still exist, though of little relevance today.
Afrocentrism	Afrocentrism is a world view that emphasizes the importance of African peoples in culture, philosophy, and history. Fundamental to Afrocentrism is the assumption that approaching knowledge from a Eurocentrist perspective, as well as certain mainstream assumptions in the application of information in the West, has led to injustices and also to inadequacies in meeting the needs of Black Africans and the peoples of the African diaspora. The Afrocentrist paradigm seeks to discover and also reinterpret information through African eyes.
Blue-collar	A blue-collar worker is a member of the working class who performs manual labor and earns an hourly wage. Blue-collar workers are distinguished from those in the service sector and from white-collar workers, whose jobs are not considered manual labor.
Blue-collar worker	A blue-collar worker is an idiom refering to a member of the working class who performs manual labor and earns an hourly wage. Blue-collar workers are distinguished from service workers and from white-collar workers, whose jobs are not considered manual labor.
Hostility	Hostility is a form of angry internal rejection or denial in psychology.
Interest	Interest is a fee paid on borrowed assets. By far the most common form these assets are lent in is money, but other assets may be lent to the borrower, such as shares, consumer goods through hire purchase, major assets such as aircraft, and even entire factories in finance lease arrangements. In each case the interest is calculated upon the value of the assets in the same manner as upon money.
Herbert J. Gans	Herbert J. Gans is an American sociologist. One of the most prolific and influential sociologists of his generation, Gans trained in urban planning at the University of Pennsylvania, where he studied with Martin Meyerson and Lewis Mumford, among others. Gans made his reputation as a critic of urban renewal in the early 1960s. His study, The Urban Villagers focused on Boston's diverse West End neighborhood which was demolished for the construction of high rise apartments. Gans contrasted the diverse, lively community of immigrants and their children with the impersonal life in the modernist towers that replaced

	them.
Nathan Glazer	Nathan Glazer is an American sociologist, who taught at UC Berkeley and Harvard University. Known for his writings on ethnicity and race, such as "Beyond the Melting Pot", co-written with Daniel Patrick Moynihan, he was an early skeptic of Great Society programs.
Helena Lopata	Helena Lopata was Professor Emeritus of Sociology at Loyola University Chicago. Her articles and book chapters covered a variety of topics, including social roles, the life course, and women's employment. She was also a 30-year member of the International Sociological Association.
Symbolic ethnicity	Ethnic identity that is retained only for symbolic importance is a symbolic ethnicity.
Paradox	A paradox can be an apparently true statement or group of statements that leads to a contradiction or a situation which defies intuition; or it can be, seemingly opposite, an apparent contradiction that actually expresses a non-dual truth.
Black Power	Black Power is a movement among Black people throughout the world, especially those in the United States. Most prominent in the late 1960s and early 1970s, the movement emphasized racial pride and the creation of black political and cultural institutions to nurture and promote black collective interests, advance black values, and secure black autonomy.
George W. Bush	George W. Bush is the forty-third and current President of the United States of America. Originally inaugurated on January 20, 2001, Bush was elected president in the 2000 presidential election and re-elected in the 2004 presidential election. He previously served as the forty-sixth Governor of Texas from 1995 to 2000.
Congress	In politics, a congress "a gathering of people" is the name of the main legislative body in a state that operates under a congressional system of government. In non-political usage congress is a term applied to a large national or international grouping of people meeting together with common interests or concerns, e.g. an academic conference.
Milton Gordon	Milton Gordon is an American sociologist. He is most noted for having devised a theory on the Seven Stages of Assimilation.
Polish American	A Polish American is an American citizen of Polish descent. There are an estimated 10 million Americans of Polish descent.
Power	Power is the ability of a person to control or influence the choices of other persons. The term authority is often used for power perceived as legitimate by the social structure. Power can be seen as evil or unjust; indeed all evil and injustice committed by man against man involve power.
Prejudice	Prejudice is, as the name implies, the process of "pre-judging" something. It implies coming to a judgment on a subject before learning where the preponderance of evidence actually lies, or forming a judgment without direct experience.
Stereotype	A stereotype is a simplified and/or standardized conception or image with specific meaning, often held in common by one group of people about another group. A stereotype can be a conventional and oversimplified conception, opinion, or image, based on the assumption that there are attributes that members of the other group hold in common. Stereotypes may be positive or negative in tone. They are typically generalizations based on minimal or limited knowledge about a group to which the person doing the stereotyping does not belong. Persons may be grouped based on race, ethnicity, religion, sexual orientation, or any number of other categories.
African Americans	African Americans are citizens or residents of the United States whose ancestors, usually in predominant part, were indigenous to Sub-Saharan Africa. Most are the descendants of captive

Africans who were enslaved within the boundaries of the present United States.

David Matza	David Matza is the Professor Emeritus in UC Berkley's Sociology Department, whose areas of interest and study include deviant behavior, social change, poverty, and working class life. He is well-known for his contributions to the field of criminology through his various publications, such as Controlling Drug Use: The Great Prohibition, Delinquency and Drift, and Becoming Deviant.
Poverty	Poverty may be seen as the collective condition of poor people, or of poor groups, and in this sense entire nation-states are sometimes regarded as poor. Although the most severe poverty is in the developing world, there is evidence of poverty in every region.
Italian American	An Italian American is an American of Italian descent. It constituted the sixth largest ancestry group in America with about 15.6 million people. An Italian American is frequently and unfairly associated with organized crime, and New York in the minds of many Americans, largely due to pervasive media stereotyping, a number of popular gangster movies.
Case study	Case study refers to a research design that focuses on a single example rather than a representative sample.
Coalition	A coalition is an alliance among entities, during which they cooperate in joint action, each in their own self-interest. This alliance may be temporary or a matter of convenience. A coalition thus differs from a more formal covenant.
Organized crime	Organized crime are groups or operations run by criminals, most commonly for the purpose of generating a monetary profit. Some organizations, such as terrorist organizations, are politically motivated. Gangs sometimes become "disciplined" enough to be considered "organized".
Social identity	In sociology and political science, the notion of social identity is individuals' labelling of themselves as members of particular groups -- such as Nation, Social class, Subculture, Ethnicity, Gender, Employment, and so forth.
Crime	A normative definition views crime as deviant behavior that violates prevailing norms, specifically, cultural standards prescribing how humans ought to behave.
Herbert Hoover	Herbert Hoover was a mining engineer and author. As the United States Secretary of Commerce in the 1920s under Presidents Warren Harding and Calvin Coolidge, he promoted government intervention under the rubric "economic modernization". In the presidential election of 1928 Hoover easily won the Republican nomination. The nation was prosperous and optimistic, leading to a landslide for Hoover over the Democrat Al Smith, whom many voters distrusted on account of his Roman Catholicism. Hoover deeply believed in the Efficiency Movement a major component of the Progressive Era, arguing that a technical solution existed for every social and economic problem.
Pluralism	Pluralism is, in the general sense, the affirmation and acceptance of diversity. Pluralism is connected with the hope that this process of conflict and dialogue will lead to a definition and subsequent realization of the common good that is best for all members of society.
Denomination	The third most powerful type of religious institution, with a membership generally dominated by a single social class, a formal but not bureaucratic role structure, a trained clergy, traditional authority, abstract relatively unemotional ritual, and a condition of coexistence between it and dominant political and economic institutions, is referred to as a denomination.
Jimmy Carter	Jimmy Carter was the thirty-ninth President of the United States from 1977 to 1981, and the Nobel Peace laureate of 2002. Prior to becoming president, Carter served two terms in the Georgia Senate, and was the 76th Governor of Georgia from 1971 to 1975.

Go to **Cram101.com** for the Practice Tests for this Chapter.

Gary Orfield	Gary Orfield is an American professor of education, law, political science and urban planning at UCLA. He s co-founder of The Civil Rights Project, to provide needed intellectual capital to academics, policy makers and civil rights advocates. His central interest is the development and implementation of social policy, with a central focus on the impact of policy on equal opportunity for success in American society.
Religion	A religion is a set of common beliefs and practices generally held by a group of people, often codified as prayer, ritual, and religious law. Religion also encompasses ancestral or cultural traditions, writings, history, and mythology, as well as personal faith and mystic experience.
Religious practices	Religious practices are the customs that are associated with a particular historical event or belief that is universally shared by a particular religious sect. Religious practices are often reminiscent of a cermony in that they are repeated procedural events that are meant to indicate devotion to an idea or deity.
Segregation	Segregation may be mandated by law or exist through social norms. Segregation may be maintained by means ranging from discrimination in hiring and in the rental and sale of housing to certain races to vigilante violence such as lynchings; a situation that arises when members of different races mutually prefer to associate and do business with members of their own race would usually be described as separation or de facto separation of the races rather than segregation.
Catholic church	The Catholic Church is the Christian church in full communion with the Bishop of Rome, currently Pope Benedict XVI. It traces its origins to the original Christian community founded by Jesus Christ and spread by the Twelve Apostles, in particular Saint Peter.
Hispanic	Hispanic is a term that historically denoted relation to the ancient Hispania and its peoples. The term now refers to the culture and people of the Spanish-speaking countries of Hispanic America and Spain; or countries with a historical legacy from Spain, including the Southwestern United States and Florida; the African nations of Equatorial Guinea, Western Sahara and the Northern coastal region of Morocco; the Asia-Pacific nations of the Philippines, Guam, Northern Mariana Islands; and to the ethnic individuals of those cultures. It can also refer to the Hispanosphere geographical distribution, the same way Latin refers to the Romance languages in general.
Hispanic American	Hispanic American is an American citizen or resident of Hispanic ethnicity and can identify themselves as having Hispanic Cultural heritage. According to the 2000 Census, Hispanics constitute the second largest ethnic group in the United States, compromizing roughly 12.5% of the population.
Life chances	Life chances are the opportunities each individual has to improve their quality of life. The concept was introduced by German sociologist Max Weber. It is a probabilistic concept, describing how likely it is, given certain factors, that an individual's life will turn out a certain way.
Pentecostals	The majority believe that one must be saved by believing in Jesus as Lord and Savior for the forgiveness of sins and to be made acceptable to God. Pentecostals also typically believe, like most other evangelicals, that the Bible has definitive authority in matters of faith. Typically, Pentecostals that do not believe speaking in tongues is necessary for salvation-- the vast majority-- are from Trinitarian traditions.
Max weber	Max Weber was a German political economist and sociologist who is considered one of the founders of the modern study of sociology and public administration. His major works deal with rationalisation in sociology of religion and government, but he also contributed much in the field of economics. His most famous work is his essay The Protestant Ethic and the Spirit of Capitalism, which began his work in the sociology of religion.

Go to **Cram101.com** for the Practice Tests for this Chapter.

Social class	Social class refers to the hierarchical distinctions between individuals or groups in societies or cultures. However, what determines class varies widely from one society to another.
Will Herberg	Will Herberg was an American Jewish writer, intellectual and scholar. He was known as a social philosopher and sociologist of religion, as well as a Jewish theologian. His essay, Protestant, Catholic, Jew, created a sociological framework for the study of religion in the United States. He demonstrated how immigration and American ethnic culture were reflected in religious movements and institutions.
Will	In common law, a will is a document by which a person regulates the rights of others over his or her property or family after death.
Robert Neely Bellah	Robert Neelly Bellah is an American sociologist, now the Elliott Professor of Sociology, Emeritus at the University of California, Berkeley.
City	A city is an urban area with a large population and a particular administrative, legal, or historical status.
Civil religion	In the sociology of religion, civil religion is the folk religion of a nation or a political culture. Professional commentators on political and social matters sometimes use the term civil religion to refer to ritual expressions of patriotism of a sort practiced in all countries, not always including religion in the conventional sense of the word.
Oklahoma City bombing	The Oklahoma City bombing was an attack on April 19, 1995 aimed at the Alfred P. Murrah Federal Building, a U.S. government office complex in downtown Oklahoma City, Oklahoma. The attack claimed 168 lives and left over 800 injured. Until the September 11, 2001 attacks, it was the deadliest act of terrorism on U.S. soil.
Americanization	Americanization is the term used for the influence the United States of America has on the culture of other countries, substituting their culture with American culture. When encountered unwillingly or perforce, it has a negative connotation; when sought voluntarily, it has a positive connotation.
Catholicism	Catholicism is a denomination of Christianity whose center is the Vatican in Rome, Italy and dates from the original church created by the Apostle Peter, a disciple of Jesus Christ.
Baptist	Baptist is a term describing individuals belonging to a Baptist church or a Baptist denomination. The name comes from the conviction that followers of Jesus Christ are commanded to be immersed in water as a public display of their faith, and thus most adherents reject infant baptism.
Rodney Stark	Rodney Stark is an American sociologist of religion. He is an advocate of the application of Rational choice theory in the sociology of religion, called theory of religious economy. His main contribution, by comparing documented evidence of Christianity's spread in the Roman Empire with the LDS church in the 19th and 20th centuries, was to illustrate that a sustained and continuous growth could lead to huge growth within 200 years.
Income	Income, generally defined, is the money that is received as a result of the normal business activities of an individual or a business.
Religious group	A religious group is a subgroup within a religion that operates under a common name, tradition, and identity.
Bigotry	A bigot is a person who is intolerant of opinions, lifestyles, or identities differing from his or her own, and bigotry is the corresponding state of mind. Forms of bigotry may have a related ideology or world views.
Christian	A Christian is a person who adheres to Christianity, a monotheistic religion centered on the life and teachings of Jesus Christ as presented in the New Testament and interpreted by

Christians to have been prophesied in the Hebrew Bible/Old Testament.

God	God is the principal or sole deity in religions and other belief systems that worship one deity.
Judaism	Judaism is the religion of the Jewish people, based on principles and ethics embodied in the Bible and the Talmud. It is among the oldest religious traditions still in practice today. While Judaism has seldom, if ever, been monolithic in practice, it has always been monotheistic in theology. It differs from many religions in that central authority is not vested in a person or group, but in sacred texts and traditions.
Orthodoxy	Orthodoxy is typically used to refer to the correct worship or the correct theological and doctrinal observance of religion, or other forms of intellectual activity shared by organizations or movements, as determined by some overseeing body
South America	South America is a continent occupying the southern part of the supercontinent of America. It sits entirely in the Western Hemisphere, and mostly in the Southern Hemisphere with a small portion in the Northern Hemisphere. It is bordered on the west by the Pacific Ocean and on the north and east by the Atlantic Ocean. North America and the Caribbean Sea lie to the northwest.
Amish	The Amish are an Anabaptist Christian denomination, formed in 1693 by Swiss Mennonites led by Jacob Amman. They live in the United States and Canada and are divided into several major groups.
Court	A court is a public forum used by a power base to adjudicate disputes and dispense civil, labor, administrative and criminal justice under its laws. In common law and civil law states, courts are the central means for dispute resolution, and it is generally understood that all persons have an ability to bring their claims before a court. Similarly, those accused of a crime have the right to present their defense before a court.
Engel v. Vitale	Engel v. Vitale was a landmark United States Supreme Court case that determined that it is unconstitutional for state officials to compose an official school prayer and require its recitation in public schools.
Lee v. Weisman	Lee v. Weisman was a United States Supreme Court decision regarding school prayer.
Court of last resort	In some countries, provinces and states, the court of last resort is the highest court whose rulings cannot be challenged.
Prayer	Prayer is the act of attempting to communicate, commonly with a sequence of words, with a deity or spirit for the purpose of worshiping, requesting guidance, confessing sins, or to express one's thoughts and emotions. The words of the prayer may take the form of a hymn, incantation, or a spontaneous utterance in the praying person's words.
Creationism	Creationism is the religious belief that humanity, life, the Earth, and the universe were created in their original form by a deity or deities, whose existence is presupposed. The wide spectrum of such beliefs includes young Earth creationism holding a very literal interpretation of Genesis, while old Earth creationism accepts geological findings but rejects evolution.
Linda Greenhouse	Linda Greenhouse a Pulitzer Prize winning reporter who covered the United States Supreme Court for three decades for the The New York Times. She has also faced criticism for expressing publicly, her personal views supporting abortion rights and criticism of US policies and actions at Guantanamo Bay, Abu Ghraib, and Haditha.
Peyote	Peyote is a small, spineless cactus whose native region extends from the southwestern United States, specifically in the southwestern part of Texas, through central Mexico.
Freedom of	Freedom of religion is a guarantee by a government for freedom of belief for individuals and

religion	freedom of worship for individuals and groups. It is generally recognized to also include the freedom not to follow any religion and not to believe in any god. Freedom of religion is considered by many in Western nations to be a fundamental human right.
Scope	In a sociological context, a scope is the state of an environment in which a situation exists. It is defined as a public place or institution where society has universally agreed that certain behaviors are considered to be acceptable while others are not.
Scopes, John	Scopes, John a teacher in Dayton, Tennessee, was charged with violating Tennessee's Butler Act, which prohibited the teaching of evolution in Tennessee schools. He was in court in a case known as the Scopes Trial.
Ritual	A ritual is a set of actions, performed mainly for their symbolic value, which is prescribed by a religion or by the traditions of a community.
Sacrifice	Sacrifice is commonly known as the practice of offering food or the lives of animals or people to the gods as an act of propitiation or worship.
Edwards v. Aguillard	Edwards v. Aguillard was a case heard by the Supreme Court of the United States. The Court ruled that a Louisiana law requiring that creation science be taught in public schools whenever evolution was taught was unconstitutional, because the law was specifically intended to advance a particular religion.
Controversy	A controversy is a matter of opinion over which parties actively disagree, argue, or debate. Controversies can range in size from private disputes between two individuals to large-scale disagreements between societies.
Groups	In sociology, a group can be defined as two or more humans that interact with one another, accept expectations and obligations as members of the group, and share a common identity. By this definition, society can be viewed as a large group, though most social groups are considerably smaller.
Lifestyle	In sociology a lifestyle is the way a person lives. This includes patterns of social relations, consumption, entertainment, and dress. A lifestyle typically also reflects an individual's attitudes, values or worldview.
Minority	A minority is a sociological group that does not constitute a politically dominant plurality of the total population of a given society. A sociological minority is not necessarily a numerical minority it may include any group that is disadvantaged with respect to a dominant group in terms of social status, education, employment, wealth and political power.
Ordnung	The Ordnung is a set of rules for Amish living.
Shunning	Shunning is the act of deliberately avoiding association with, and habitually keeping away from an individual or group. It is a sanction against association often associated with religious groups and other tightly-knit organisations and communities. Targets of shunning can include, but are not limited to apostates, whistleblowers, dissidents, people classified as "sinners" or "traitors" and other people who defy or who fail to comply with the standards established by the shunning groups. Shunning has a long history as a means of organisational influence and control. Extreme forms of shunning and related practices have rendered the general practice controversial in some circles.
Society	A society is a grouping of individuals, which is characterized by common interest and may have distinctive culture and institutions.
Understanding	Understanding is a psychological process related to an abstract or physical object, such as, person, situation, or message whereby one is able to think about it and use concepts to deal adequately with that object.
Child labor	Child labor is the employment of children under an age determined by law or custom. This

practice is considered exploitative by many countries and international organizations. Child labor was not seen as a problem throughout most of history, only becoming a disputed issue with the beginning of universal schooling and the concepts of laborers and children's rights.

Labor force

In economics the people in the labor force are the suppliers of labor. The fraction of the labor force that is seeking work but cannot find it determines the unemployment rate. The labor force participation rate is the ratio between the labor force and the overall size of their cohort.

Wisconsin

Wisconsin is a state located near the center of the North American continent. It touches two of the five Great Lakes and is one of the fifty states that constitute the United States of America. Wisconsin's capital is Madison, and its largest city is Milwaukee. Jim Doyle has been the Governor of Wisconsin since January 6, 2003.

Labor

In economics, labor is a measure of the work done by human beings. It is conventionally contrasted with such other factors of production as land and capital. There are theories which have created a concept called human capital, although there are also counter posing macro-economic system theories that think human capital is a contradiction in terms.

Donald B. Kraybill

Donald B. Kraybill is a prolific author, lecturer, and educator on Anabaptist faiths and living. Kraybill is widely recognized for his studies on Anabaptist groups, and is the foremost living expert on the Old Order Amish.

Go to **Cram101.com** for the Practice Tests for this Chapter.
And, **NEVER** highlight a book again!

Native Americans	Native Americans in the United States are the indigenous peoples from the regions of North America now encompassed by the continental United States, including parts of Alaska. They comprise a large number of distinct tribes, states, and ethnic groups, many of which are
Navajo	Navajo refers or relates to the Navajo people, the second largest Native American tribe in the United States.
Language	A language is a system of symbols and the rules used to manipulate them. Language can also refer to the use of such systems as a general phenomenon. Because a language also has a grammar, it can manipulate its symbols to express clear and regular relationships between them.
Population	A population is the collection of people or organisms of a particular species living in a given geographic area or space, usually measured by a census.
Resistance	Psychological resistance is the phenomenon often encountered in clinical practice in which patients either directly or indirectly oppose changing their behavior or refuse to discuss, remember, or think about presumably clinically relevant experiences.
Tribal society	Tribal society refers to societies organized largely on the basis of kinship, especially corporate descent groups. It means a social division within a traditional society consisting of a group of interlinked families or communities sharing a common culture and dialect.
Columbus, Christopher	Columbus, Christopher was a navigator, colonizer and one of the first Europeans to explore the Americas after the Vikings. Though not the first to reach the Americas from Europe, it was his voyages that led to general European awareness of the hemisphere and the successful establishment of European cultures in the New World.
Vine Deloria	Vine Deloria was an American Indian author, theologian, historian, and activist. His most famous work is Custer Died for Your Sins: An Indian Manifesto. In it, he addressed Indian stereotypes and challenged white audiences to take a new look at the history of American western expansionism.
Contact	In Family Law, contact is one of the general terms which denotes the level of contact a parent or other significant person in a child's life can have with that child. Contact forms part of the bundle of rights and privileges which a parent may have in relation to any child of the family.
Culture	Culture generally refers to patterns of human activity and the symbolic structures that give such activity significant importance. Culture has been called "the way of life for an entire society." As such, it includes codes of manners, dress, language, religion, rituals, norms of behavior such as law and morality, and systems of belief.
Bureau of Indian Affairs	The Bureau of Indian Affairs is an agency of the federal government of the United States within the Department of the Interior charged with the administration and management of 55.7 million acres of land held in trust by the United States for American Indians, Indian tribes and Alaska Natives. In addition, the Bureau of Indian Affairs provides education services to approximately 48,000 Indians.
Christopher Chase-Dunn	Christopher Chase-Dunn is Professor of Sociology and Director of the Institute for Research on World-Systems at the University of California-Riverside. He is also the founder of the electronic Journal of World-Systems Research.
C. Matthew Snipp	C. Matthew Snipp is Professor of Sociology at the Stanford University. His work focuses on discovering there is a great deal of volatility in the reporting of race by persons of American Indian ancestry. His project consists of census data that were especially collected using several different variations of a question designed to elicit information about racial identification.

Go to **Cram101.com** for the Practice Tests for this Chapter.

Cheyenne	Cheyenne are a Native American nation of the Great Plains. When the Cheyenne were fully adapted to the classic Plains culture, they had a bi-lateral band kinship system. However, some anthropologists note that the Cheyenne had a matrilineal band system.
Chickasaw	The Chickasaw are Native American people originally from the Southeastern United States. They are of the Muskogean linguistic group. The Chickasaws were one of the "Five Civilized Tribes" who sold their country and moved to Indian Territory during the era of Indian Removal. The Chickasaw Nation in Oklahoma is the thirteenth largest federally-recognized tribe in the United States.
Choctaw	The Choctaw are a Native American people originally from the Southeastern United States. They are of the Muskogean linguistic group. Choctaw culture has greatly evolved over the centuries combining mostly European-American influences; however, interaction with Spain, France, and England greatly shaped it as well. They were known for their rapid incorporation of modernity, developing a written language, transitioning to yeoman farming methods, and accepting European-Americans and African-Americans into their society.
Cloud	A cloud is a visible mass of droplets or frozen crystals floating in the atmosphere above the surface of the Earth or another planetary body.
Creek	The Creek are an American Indian people originally from the southeastern United States, also known by their original name Muscogee, the name they use to identify themselves today. More of a loose confederacy than a single tribe, the Muscogee lived in autonomous villages in river valleys throughout what are today the states of Tennessee, Georgia, and Alabama and consisted of many ethnic groups speaking several distinct languages, such as the Hitchiti, Alabama, and Coushatta.
Indian Removal Act	The Indian Removal Act was signed into law by President Andrew Jackson on May 28, 1830. This Act was strongly supported in the South, where states were eager to gain access to lands inhabited by the "Five Civilized Tribes".
Red Cloud	Red Cloud was a war leader of the Oglala Lakota Sioux. One of the most capable Native American opponents the U. S. military ever faced, he led a successful conflict in 1866–1868 known as Red Cloud's War over control of the Powder River Country in northwestern Wyoming and southern Montana. Later, he led his people in reservation life.
Seminole	The Seminole are a Native American people originally of Florida and now residing in Florida and Oklahoma. They have sovereignty over their tribal lands and an economy based on tobacco sales, tourism, and gambling and entertainment. The Seminole nation was formed in the 18th century and was composed of Native Americans from Georgia, Mississippi, and Alabama, most significantly the Creek Nation, as well as African Americans who escaped to Florida from slavery in South Carolina and Georgia.
Trail of Tears	The Trail of Tears refers to the forced relocation in 1838 of the Cherokee Native American tribe to Indian Territory in what would be the state of Oklahoma, resulting in the deaths of an estimated 4,000 of the 15,000 Cherokees affected. This was caused by the "Indian Removal Act of 1830".
Ethnic identity	Ethnic identity refers to an enduring, basic aspect of the self that includes a sense of membership in an ethnic group and the attitudes and feelings related to that membership. Ethnic identity can vary with changes in social context.
Identity	Identity is an umbrella term used throughout the social sciences to describe an individual's comprehension of him or herself as a discrete, separate entity.
Ghost Dance	Noted in historical accounts as the Ghost Dance of 1890, the Ghost Dance was a religious movement incorporated into numerous Native American belief systems. The traditional ritual used in the Ghost Dance, the circle dance, has been used by many Native Americans since pre-

	historic times, but was first performed in accordance with Jack Wilson's teachings among the Nevada Paiute in 1889.
Pine Ridge Reservation	Pine Ridge Reservation is an Oglala Sioux Native American reservation located in the U.S. state of South Dakota. Pine Ridge was established in the southwest corner of South Dakota on the Nebraska border and consists of 8,984.306 km² of land area, the eighth-largest reservation in the United States, larger than Delaware and Rhode Island combined.
Plains Indians	The Plains Indians are the Indians who lived on the plains and rolling hills of the Great Plains of North America.
Internal colonialism	Internal Colonialism refers to political and economic inequalities between regions within a single society. The term may be used to describe the uneven effects of state development on a regional basis and to describe the exploitation of minority groups within the wider society.
Jessica Dawn Lynch	Jessica Dawn Lynch is a former Quartermaster Corps Private First Class in the United States Army.
Colonialism	Colonialism is the extension of a nation's sovereignty over territory beyond its borders by the establishment of either settler colonies or administrative dependencies in which indigenous populations are directly ruled or displaced.
Indian Reorganization Act	The Indian Reorganization Act was a U.S. federal legislation which secured certain rights to Native Americans, including Alaska Natives.
Policy	A policy is a deliberate plan of action to guide decisions and achieve rational outcomes. The term may apply to government, private sector organizations and groups, and individuals. Presidential executive orders, corporate privacy policies, and parliamentary rules of order are all examples of policy. Policy differs from rules or law. While law can compel or prohibit behaviors policy merely guides actions toward those that are most likely to achieve a desired outcome.
Indian Claims Commission	The Indian Claims Commission was a panel for relations between the United States Federal Government and Native American tribes.
Court	A court is a public forum used by a power base to adjudicate disputes and dispense civil, labor, administrative and criminal justice under its laws. In common law and civil law states, courts are the central means for dispute resolution, and it is generally understood that all persons have an ability to bring their claims before a court. Similarly, those accused of a crime have the right to present their defense before a court.
Joane Nagel	Joane Nagel is Professor of Sociology of the University of Kansas. She serves as the director of KU's Center for Research on Global Change within the Institute for Policy and Social Research, where she works in the social and natural sciences in engineering to design a graduate training program in Climate Change. Her research focuses on the politics of ethnciity and sexuality.
John Collier	John Collier was an American social reformer and Native American advocate. He made his first significant contribution to a national magazine when an article which described the socialist municipal government in Milwaukee, Wisconsin was published in Harper's Weekly. He centered his career on trying to realize the power of social institutions to make and modify personalities.
Urbanization	Urbanization is the increase over time in the population of cities in relation to the region's rural population. Urbanization has intense effects on the ecology of a region and on its economy.
Pan-Indianism	Pan-Indianism is an intertribal movement of native resistance to white domination and

Go to **Cram101.com** for the Practice Tests for this Chapter.

	assimilation. It is characterized primarily by political and religious expressions and solidarity. Key historical figures incldue Pontiac and Handsome Lake. Pan-Indianism is a non-violent liberation philosophy with roots in Native.
Collective action	Collective action is the pursuit of a goal or set of goals by more than one person.
American Indian Movement	The American Indian Movement, is an Indian activist organization in the United States.
American Indians	American Indians are the indigenous peoples from the regions of North America now encompassed by the continental United States, including parts of Alaska. They comprise a large number of distinct tribes, states, and ethnic groups, many of which survive as intact political communities. There has been a wide range of terms used to describe them and no consensus has been reached among indigenous members as to what they prefer.
Congress	In politics, a congress "a gathering of people" is the name of the main legislative body in a state that operates under a congressional system of government. In non-political usage congress is a term applied to a large national or international grouping of people meeting together with common interests or concerns, e.g. an academic conference.
Iroquois	The Iroquois Confederacy is a group of First Nations/Native Americans that originally consisted of five tribes: the Mohawk, the Oneida, the Onondaga, the Cayuga, and the Seneca. A sixth tribe, the Tuscarora, joined after the original five nations were formed.
Medicine	Medicine is the practice of maintaining and restoring human health through the study, diagnosis, and treatment of patients whose death it is the discipline's ultimate concern to avert. It has traditionally been regarded as both an art and a science: the term is derived from the Latin ars medicina meaning the art of healing.
National Congress of American Indians	The National Congress of American Indians is a Native American organization based in the United States.
Bushmen	The Bushmen are indigenous people of the Kalahari Desert, which spans areas of South Africa, Botswana, Namibia and Angola. They were traditionally hunter-gatherers, part of the Khoisan group, and are related to the traditionally pastoral Khoikhoi. Genetic evidence suggests they are one of the oldest, if not the oldest, peoples in the world.
Treaty of Medicine Creek	The Treaty of Medicine Creek was an 1854 treaty between the Washington Territory, the United States, and the Nisqually, Puyallup and Squaxin Island tribes, along with six other smaller Native American tribes.
Protest	Protest expresses relatively overt reaction to events or situations: sometimes in favor, though more often opposed. Protesters may organize a protest as a way of publicly and forcefully making their opinions heard in an attempt to influence public opinion or government policy, or may undertake direct action to attempt to directly enact desired changes themselves.
Inuit	Inuit is a general term for a group of culturally similar indigenous peoples inhabiting the Arctic regions of Alaska, Greenland, the Canadian territories of Northwest Territories and Nunavut, the province of Quebec and the northern part of Labrador.
Justice	Justice concerns the proper ordering of things and persons within a society. As a concept it has been subject to philosophical, legal, and theological reflection and debate throughout history.
Power	Power is the ability of a person to control or influence the choices of other persons. The

term authority is often used for power perceived as legitimate by the social structure. Power can be seen as evil or unjust; indeed all evil and injustice committed by man against man involve power.

Red Power movement	Red Power movement, attributed to Vine Deloria Jr., commonly expressed a growing sense of pan-Indian identity
Thunderheart	Thunderheart is a 1992 American crime film directed by Michael Apted with Val Kilmer, Sam Shepard, Graham Greene, and Fred Ward.
Russell Means	Russell Means is one of contemporary America's best-known and prolific activists for the rights of American Indians. He traveled to Nicaragua to express his support for Miskito Indians who were allied with the US-funded contra guerillas against the Nicaraguan government.
Overview	An overview in policy debate is part of a speech which is flagged as not responding to the line-by-line arguments on the flow. An overview may be "global" if presented at the beginning of a speech or "local" if presented at the beginning of a position.
Sovereignty	Sovereignty is the exclusive right to exercise supreme political (e.g. legislative, judicial, and/or executive) authority over a geographic region, group of people, or oneself.
Economic development	Economic development is the development of the economic wealth of countries or regions for the well-being of their inhabitants. Economic development is a sustainable increase in living standards that implies increased per capita income, better education and health as well as environmental protection.
Gambling	The term gambling in Western societies, has an economic definition, referring to "wagering money or something of material value on an event with an uncertain outcome with the primary intent of winning additional money and/or material goods". Typically the outcome of the wager is evident within a short period of time.
Indian Gaming Regulatory Act	The Indian Gaming Regulatory Act is a 1988 United States federal law which establishes the jurisdictional framework that presently governs Indian gaming.
James B. Steele	James B. Steele is an American investigative journalist and author. In a collaboration for The Philadelphia Inquirer, James B. Steele and Donald L. Barlett pioneered the use of computers for the analysis of data on violent crimes. Twenty years later, they co-authored the series America: What Went Wrong? for The Inquirer, which was named as one of the 100 best pieces of journalism of the 20th century by the New York University School of Journalism.
Full Employment	A situation in which everyone or nearly everyone who wants to work can find a job is full employment.
Morton v. Mancari	Morton v. Mancari was a case about the constitutionality, under the Fifth Amendment, of hiring preferences given to Indians within the Bureau of Indian Affairs.
Government	A government is a body that has the authority to make and the power to enforce laws within a civil, corporate, religious, academic, or other organization or group.
Poverty	Poverty may be seen as the collective condition of poor people, or of poor groups, and in this sense entire nation-states are sometimes regarded as poor. Although the most severe poverty is in the developing world, there is evidence of poverty in every region.
Unemployment	Unemployment is the condition of willing workers lacking jobs or "gainful employment". A key measure is the unemployment rate, which is the number of unemployed workers divided by the total civilian labor force.
Oneida	The Oneida are a Native American/First Nations people and are one of the five founding nations of the Iroquois Confederacy in the area of upstate New York.

Sequoyah	Sequoyah was a Cherokee silversmith who invented the Cherokee syllabary.
James Coleman	James Coleman was a sociological theorist, who studied the sociology of education, public policy, and was one of the earliest users of the term "social capital". His Foundations of Social Theory stands as one of the most important sociological contributions of the late-20th century.
Pushout	A pushout is a student counseled or forced out of a school prior to graduation.
Risk	Risk is a concept that denotes a potential negative impact to some characteristic of value that may arise from a future event, or we can say that "Risks are events or conditions that may occur, and whose occurrence, if it does take place, has a harmful or negative effect". Exposure to the consequences of uncertainty constitutes a risk. In everyday usage, risk is often used synonymously with the probability of a known loss.
Silberman	Silberman uses econometric methods to measure the effectiveness in terms of criminal deterrence of two factors: the degree of punishment; and the probability of apprehension. A simple "expected loss" model would predict that deterrent effect would depend only on the result of multiplying the penalty by the probability of it occurring. Silberman concluded that contrary to this model, the likelihood of punishment had a greater effect in most situations.
Higher education	Higher education is education provided by universities, vocational universities and other collegial institutions that award academic degrees, such as career colleges. Higher education includes teaching, research and social services activities of universities, and within the realm of teaching, it includes both the undergraduate level and the graduate level.
Community	A community is a social group of organisms sharing an environment, normally with shared interests. In human communities, intent, belief, resources, preferences, needs, risks and a number of other conditions may be present and common, affecting the identity of the participants and their degree of cohesiveness.
Public Health	Public health is concerned with threats to the overall health of a community based on population health analysis.
Public Health Service	The Public Health Service is the primary division of the United States Department of Health and Human Services that is focused on the protection, promotion, and advancement of public health. It is is comprised of all Agency Divisions of Health and Human Services and the Commissioned Corps. The Assistant Secretary for Health oversees the PHS and the United States Public Health.
Health care	Health care is the prevention, treatment, and management of illness and the preservation of mental and physical well being through the services offered by the medical, nursing, and allied health professions. In most developed countries and many developing countries health care is provided to everyone regardless of their ability to pay. The health care industry is one of the world's largest and fastest-growing industries.
Tradition	Tradition can be a practice, custom, or story that is memorized and passed down from generation to generation, originally without the need for a writing system.
Natalie Angier	Natalie Angier is a nonfiction writer and a science journalist for the New York Times. She also worked as a science writer for Time Magazine, and was briefly an adjunct professor in New York University's Graduate Program in Science, Health and Environmental Reporting.
Freedom of religion	Freedom of religion is a guarantee by a government for freedom of belief for individuals and freedom of worship for individuals and groups. It is generally recognized to also include the freedom not to follow any religion and not to believe in any god. Freedom of religion is considered by many in Western nations to be a fundamental human right.

Religious practices	Religious practices are the customs that are associated with a particular historical event or belief that is universally shared by a particular religious sect. Religious practices are often reminiscent of a cermony in that they are repeated procedural events that are meant to indicate devotion to an idea or deity.
Burgess	Burgess is an English word that originally meant a freeman of a borough or burgh.
Ernest Burgess	Ernest Burgess was an urban sociologist. His groundbreaking social ecology research, in conjunction with his colleague, Robert E. Park, provided the foundation for The Chicago School. In The City, they conceptualized the city into the concentric zones, including the central business district, transitional, working class residential, residential, and commuter/suburban zones.
Hopi	The Hopi are a Native American people who primarily live on the 6,557.262 km² Hopi Reservation in northeastern Arizona. Hopi is a concept deeply rooted in the culture's religion, spirituality, and its view of morality and ethics. Traditionally, they are organized into matrilineal clans.
Peyote	Peyote is a small, spineless cactus whose native region extends from the southwestern United States, specifically in the southwestern part of Texas, through central Mexico.
J. P. Martin	J. P. Martin was an English author best known for his Uncle series of children's stories.
Peyotism	Peyotism, originated in the U.S. state of Oklahoma, and is the most widespread indigenous religion among Native Americans. Peyotism involves the use of the entheogen Peyote, a spineless cactus.
Apache	Apache is the collective name for several culturally related groups of Native Americans in the United States. These indigenous peoples of North America speak a Southern Athabaskan language, and are related linguistically to the Athabaskan speakers of Alaska and western Canada. The present-day Apache groups include the Jicarilla and Mescalero of New Mexico, the Chiricahua of the Arizona-New Mexico border area, the Western Apache of Arizona, the Lipan Apache of southwestern Texas, and the Plains Apache of Oklahoma.
Canyonlands National Park	Canyonlands National Park is located in the American state of Utah, near city of Moab and preserves a colorful landscape eroded into countless canyons, mesas and buttes by the Colorado River and its tributaries.
Environmental justice	Environmental justice is a term in the social sciences used to describe injustices in the way natural resources are used. Environmental justice is a holistic effort to analyze and overcome the power structures that have traditionally thwarted environmental reforms.
Grand Canyon National Park	Grand Canyon National Park is one of the United States' oldest national parks and is located in Arizona.
Park	A park is a bounded area of land, usually in its natural or semi-natural landscaped state and set aside for some purpose, usually to do with recreation.
Controversy	A controversy is a matter of opinion over which parties actively disagree, argue, or debate. Controversies can range in size from private disputes between two individuals to large-scale disagreements between societies.

84

Go to **Cram101.com** for the Practice Tests for this Chapter.

African Americans	African Americans are citizens or residents of the United States whose ancestors, usually in predominant part, were indigenous to Sub-Saharan Africa. Most are the descendants of captive Africans who were enslaved within the boundaries of the present United States.
Immigration	Although human migration has existed for hundreds of thousands of years, immigration in the modern sense refers to movement of people from one nation-state to another, where they are not citizens.
Martin Luther King, Jr.	Martin Luther King, Jr. was a leader in the American civil rights movement. King was a Baptist minister, one of the few leadership roles available to black men at the time. He became a civil rights activist early in his career. He led the Montgomery Bus Boycott and helped found the Southern Christian Leadership Conference, serving as its first president. His efforts led to the 1963 March on Washington, where King delivered his "I Have a Dream"
Luther, Martin	Luther, Martin was a German monk, theologian, and church reformer. He is also considered to be the founder of Protestantism. . According to him, salvation was attainable only by faith in Jesus as the Messiah, a faith unmediated by the church. These ideas helped to inspire the Protestant Reformation and changed the course of Western civilization. He is also known for his writings about the Jews, the nature and consequences of which are the subject of scholarly debate.
Slavery	Slavery refers to an extreme form of stratification in which some people are owned by others.
Population	A population is the collection of people or organisms of a particular species living in a given geographic area or space, usually measured by a census.
Stanley Elkins	Stanley Elkins is the Sydenham Clark Parsons Professor Emeritus of history at Smith College. He made two major, and controversial, arguments in Slavery. The first was that American abolitionists undercut their own effectiveness by their insistence on ideological consistency and purity, and their refusal to compromise with the slave system. His second argument was that the experience of slavery was psychologically infantilizing to slaves. He based his arguments on recent sociological and psychological research by Bruno Bettelheim and others on inmates of German concentration camps during World War II.
John Hope Franklin	John Hope Franklin is a United States historian and past president of the American Historical Association. Professor Emeritus of History at Duke University, he is best known for his work From Slavery to Freedom. He was an early beneficiary of the fraternity's Foundation Publishers which provides financial support and fellowship for writers addressing African American issues.
Marriage	A marriage is an interpersonal relationship with governmental, social, or religious recognition, usually intimate and sexual, and often created as a contract. The most frequently occurring form of marriage unites a man and a woman as husband and wife. Other forms of marriage also exist; for example, polygamy, in which a person takes more than one spouse, is common in many societies
Religion	A religion is a set of common beliefs and practices generally held by a group of people, often codified as prayer, ritual, and religious law. Religion also encompasses ancestral or cultural traditions, writings, history, and mythology, as well as personal faith and mystic experience.
Christianity	Christianity is a monotheistic religion and a relationship centered on the life and teachings of Jesus of Nazareth as depicted in the New Testament. With one estimate implying 2.1 billion adherents, or approximately 33% of the world's population in 2007, Christianity is the world's largest religion. It is the predominant religion in Europe, the Americas, Southern Africa, the Philippines and Oceania.
William Edward	William Edward Burghardt Du Bois was an African American civil rights activist, public

Burghardt Du Bois	intellectual, Pan-Africanist, sociologist, educator, historian, writer, editor, poet, and scholar. He became a naturalized citizen of Ghana in 1963 at the age of 95.
Douglass, Frederick	Douglass, Frederick was an American abolitionist, editor, orator, author, statesman and reformer. He was a firm believer in the equality of all people, whether black, female, American Indian, or recent immigrant. He devoted his life to advocating the brotherhood of all humankind. He was fond of saying, "I would unite with anybody to do right and with nobody to do wrong."
Language	A language is a system of symbols and the rules used to manipulate them. Language can also refer to the use of such systems as a general phenomenon. Because a language also has a grammar, it can manipulate its symbols to express clear and regular relationships between them.
Truth	The meaning of the word truth extends from honesty, good faith, and sincerity in general, to agreement with fact or reality in particular. The term has no single definition about which the majority of professional philosophers and scholars agree. Various theories of truth continue to be debated. There are differing claims on such questions as what constitutes truth; how to define and identify truth; the roles that revealed and acquired knowledge play; and whether truth is subjective, relative, objective, or absolute.
Berlin	Berlin is the capital city and one of sixteen states of Germany. With a population of 3.4 million within its city limits, Berlin is the country's largest city. It is the second most populous city and the ninth most populous urban area in the European Union.[2] Located in northeastern Germany, it is the centre of the Berlin-Brandenburg metropolitan area, comprising 5 million people from over 180 nations.[3]
Constitution	A constitution is a system, often codified as a written document, that establishes the rules and principles that govern an organization or political entity. In the case of countries, this term refers specifically to a national constitution defining the fundamental political principles, and establishing the structure, procedures, powers and duties, of a government.
Crow	The Crow are a tribe of Native Americans who historically lived in the Yellowstone River valley and now live on a reservation south of Billings, Montana. Traditional clothing the Crow wore depended on gender. Women tended to wear simple clothes. Male clothing usually consisted of a shirt, trimmed leggings with a belt, a robe, and moccasins. Women held a very significant role within the tribe.
Emancipation	Emancipation is a term used to describe various efforts to obtain political rights or equality, often for a specifically disenfranchised group, or more generally in discussion of such matters.
Emancipation Proclamation	The Emancipation Proclamation consists of two executive orders issued by United States President Abraham Lincoln during the American Civil War. It was widely attacked at the time as freeing only the slaves over which the Union had no power, but in practice, it committed the Union to ending slavery, which was controversial in the North.
Fifteenth Amendment	Fifteenth Amendment of the United States Constitution provides that governments in the United States may not prevent a citizen from voting because of his race, color, or previous condition of servitude.
Jim Crow laws	The Jim Crow Laws were state and local laws enacted in the Southern and border states of the United States. They mandated "separate but equal" status for black Americans. In reality, this led to treatment and accommodations that were almost always inferior to those provided to white Americans.
Union League	A Union League is one of a number of organizations established in 1863 and 1864 during the American Civil War to promote loyalty to the Union side and the policies of Abraham Lincoln.

Plessy v. Ferguson	Plessy v. Ferguson, 163 U.S. 537, was a landmark United States Supreme Court decision in the jurisprudence of the United States, upholding the constitutionality of racial segregation even in public accommodations, under the doctrine of "separate but equal".
Poll tax	A poll tax is a tax of a uniform, fixed amount per individual.
Separate but equal	Separate but equal is a phrase used to describe a system of segregation, where people of different ethnic backgrounds (or, in practice, people simply perceived to be different from each other in a manner considered significant enough to justify segregationist policies or practices) have the same qualitative and quantitative rights to services and facilities, but receive them apart from each other.
Underground Railroad	The Underground Railroad was a network of secret routes and safe houses that 19th century African slaves in the United States used to escape to free states with the aid of abolitionists.
Voting	Voting is a method of decision making wherein a group such as a meeting or an electorate attempts to gauge its opinion—usually as a final step following discussions or debates.
White supremacy	White supremacy is a racist paradigm based on the assertion that white people are superior to other races. The term is sometimes used specifically to describe a political ideology that advocates social and political dominance for whites.
Williams v. Mississippi	Williams v. Mississippi is a United States Supreme Court case that reviewed provisions of the state constitution that set requirements for voter registration.
Institutiona-ization	The term institutionalization is widely used in social theory to denote the process of making something (for example a concept, a social role, particular values and norms, or modes of behavior) become embedded within an organization, social system, or society as an established custom or norm within that system.
Segregation	Segregation may be mandated by law or exist through social norms. Segregation may be maintained by means ranging from discrimination in hiring and in the rental and sale of housing to certain races to vigilante violence such as lynchings; a situation that arises when members of different races mutually prefer to associate and do business with members of their own race would usually be described as separation or de facto separation of the races rather than segregation.
John Conyers	John Conyers is a member of the United States House of Representatives representing Michigan's 14th congressional district, which includes all of Highland Park and Hamtramck, as well as parts of Detroit and Dearborn. A Democrat, he has served since 1965. In January 2007, Conyers became chairman of the House Judiciary Committee in the 110th United States Congress.Conyers is currently the second-longest serving member of the House and the fifth member of entire Congress by length of service. He is married to Monica Conyers, who is a member of the Detroit City Council.
Lincoln, Abraham	Lincoln, Abraham was the sixteenth President of the United States. During his term, he helped preserve the United States by leading the defeat of the secessionist Confederate States of America in the American Civil War. He introduced measures that resulted in the abolition of slavery, issuing his Emancipation Proclamation and promoting the passage of the Thirteenth Amendment to the Constitution.
Legislation	Legislation is law which has been promulgated by a legislature or other governing body. The term may refer to a single law, or the collective body of enacted law, while "statute" is also used to refer to a single law. Before an item of legislation becomes law it may be known as a bill, which is typically also known as "legislation" while it remains under active consideration.
Insurance	Insurance, in law and economics, is a form of risk management primarily used to hedge against

the risk of a contingent loss. Insurance is defined as the equitable transfer of the risk of a loss, from one entity to another, in exchange for a premium. An insurer is a company selling the insurance. The insurance rate is a factor used to determine the amount, called the premium, to be charged for a certain amount of insurance coverage. Risk management, the practice of appraising and controlling risk, has evolved as a discrete field of study and practice.

Washington	Washington is a state in the Pacific Northwest region of the United States. Named after George Washington, it is the only U.S. state named after a president.
Booker T. Washington	Booker T. Washington was an American educator, author and leader of the African American community. He was freed from slavery as a child, gained an education, and as a young man was appointed to lead a teachers' college for blacks. From this position of leadership he rose into a nationally prominent role as spokesman for African Americans.
Patricia J. Williams	Patricia J. Williams is a prominent law critic and a proponent of critical race theory, an offshoot of 1960s social movements that emphasizes race as a fundamental determinant of the American legal system. She also worked as a consumer advocate in the office of the City Attorney in Los Angeles.
Labor	In economics, labor is a measure of the work done by human beings. It is conventionally contrasted with such other factors of production as land and capital. There are theories which have created a concept called human capital, although there are also counter posing macro-economic system theories that think human capital is a contradiction in terms.
Leadership	Leadership is the ability to affect human behavior so as to accomplish a mission designated by the leader. Most research into leadership mistakenly focused on cognitive and intellectual processes, forgetting the important fact that every cognitive process is an embodied process.
Accommodation	Accommodation is a linguistics term meaning grammatical acceptance of unstated values as in Accommodation of presuppositions.
Niagara Movement	The Niagara Movement was a civil rights organization founded in 1905 by a group led by W. E. B. Du Bois and William Monroe Trotter.
Politics	Politics is the process by which groups of people make decisions. Although the term is generally applied to behavior within governments, politics is observed in all human group interactions, including corporate, academic, and religious institutions.
Lynching	Lynching is a form of violence, usually execution, conceived of by its perpetrators as extrajudicial punishment for offenders or as a terrorist method of enforcing social domination. It is characterized by a summary procedure ignoring, bypassing, or even contrary to, the strict forms of law, notably judicial execution.
National Association for the Advancement of Colored People	The National Association for the Advancement of Colored People is one of the oldest and most influential radical civil rights organizations in the United States. It was founded on February 12, 1909 by a diverse group composed of W.E.B. Du Bois, Ida Wells-Barnett, Henry Moskowitz, Mary White Ovington, Oswald Garrison Villard, and William English Walling, to work on behalf of the rights of African Americans. Its name, retained in accord with tradition, is one of the last surviving uses of the term "colored people." The group is based in Baltimore, Maryland.
Migration	The movement of people from one country or region to another in order to settle permanently, is referred to as a migration.
Violence	Violence is, on the one hand, acts of aggression and abuse that cause' or intend to cause injury to person or persons. Central to this concept of violence is the presence of the definite intention to cause significant injury, damage and harm.

Go to **Cram101.com** for the Practice Tests for this Chapter.

Go to **Cram101.com** for the Practice Tests for this Chapter.
And, **NEVER** highlight a book again!

Ku Klux Klan	Ku Klux Klan is the name of several past and present organizations in the United States that have advocated white supremacy, antisemitism, racism, homophobia, and nativism. These organizations have often used terrorism, violence and acts of intimidation, such as cross lighting to oppress African Americans, and other social or ethnic groups.
Military	Military has two broad meanings. In its first sense, it refers to soldiers and soldiering. In its second sense, it refers to armed forces as a whole.
A. Philip Randolph	A. Philip Randolph was a prominent twentieth century African-American civil rights leader and founder of the Brotherhood of Sleeping Car Porters, which was a huge achievement for labor and especially for African-American labor organizing.
Protest	Protest expresses relatively overt reaction to events or situations: sometimes in favor, though more often opposed. Protesters may organize a protest as a way of publicly and forcefully making their opinions heard in an attempt to influence public opinion or government policy, or may undertake direct action to attempt to directly enact desired changes themselves.
Congress	In politics, a congress "a gathering of people" is the name of the main legislative body in a state that operates under a congressional system of government. In non-political usage congress is a term applied to a large national or international grouping of people meeting together with common interests or concerns, e.g. an academic conference.
Congress of Racial Equality	The Congress of Racial Equality is a U.S. civil rights organization that played a pivotal role in the Civil Rights Movement from its foundation to the mid-1960s. The group's inspiration was Krishnalal Shridharani's book War Without Violence, which outlined Gandhi's step-by-step procedures for organizing people and mounting a nonviolent campaign.
Freedom riders	Civil Rights activists called Freedom Riders rode in interstate buses into the segregated southern United States to test the United States Supreme Court decision Boynton v. Virginia, 364 U.S. The first Freedom Ride left Washington D.C. on May 4, 1961, and was scheduled to arrive in New Orleans on May 17. Riders were arrested for trespassing, unlawful assembly, violating state and local Jim Crow laws, etc.
Garfinkel	Garfinkel is one of the key developers of the phenomenological tradition in American sociology. His own development of this tradition (which he terms ethnomethodology) is widely misunderstood. In contrast to the social constructionist version of phenomenological sociology, he emphasises a focus on radical phenomena, rather than on the various ways they are interpretated.
Restrictive covenant	A restrictive covenant is a legal obligation imposed in a deed by the seller upon the buyer of real estate to do or not to do something. Such restrictions frequently "run with the land" and are enforceable on subsequent buyers of the property. Some are very simple and are meant only to protect a neighborhood from homeowners destroying trees or historic things or otherwise directly harming property values.
Shelley v. Kramer	Shelley v. Kramer is a United States Supreme Court decision involving the enforceability of restrictive covenants which would prohibit a person from owning or occupying property on the basis of race. It is an important civil rights case.
Smith v. Allwright	Smith v. Allwright was an important decision of the United States Supreme Court with regard to voting rights and, by extension, racial desegregation.
Brown v. Board of Education	Brown v. Board of Education was a landmark decision of the United States Supreme Court, which overturned earlier rulings going back to Plessy v. Ferguson in 1896, by declaring that state laws which established separate public schools for black and white students denied black children equal educational opportunities.
Civil Rights	Civil rights are the protections and privileges of personal liberty given to all citizens by

law. Civil rights are rights that are bestowed by nations on those within their territorial boundaries.

Civil Rights Movement	Historically, the civil rights movement was a concentrated period of time around the world of approximately one generation (1954-1980) wherein there was much worldwide civil unrest and popular rebellion.
De jure	De jure is an expression that means "based on law". The phrase is often used in the context of American desegregation legislation. Codified segregation is de jure segregation.
De jure segregation	De jure segregation in both South Africa and the U.S. came with "miscegenation laws" (prohibitions against interracial marriage) and laws against hiring people of the race that is the object of discrimination in any but menial positions.
Desegregation	Desegregation is the process of ending racial segregation, most commonly used in reference to the United States. Desegregation was long a focus of the American Civil Rights Movement, both before and after the United States Supreme Court's decision in Brown v. Board of Education, particularly desegregation of the school systems and the military, as was the closely related but somewhat more ambitious goal of racial integration.
Assimilation	A minority group's internalization of the values and norms of the dominant culture is referred to as assimilation.
Fourteenth Amendment	The Fourteenth Amendment Amendment XIV to the United States Constitution is one of the post-Civil War amendments known as the Reconstruction Amendments, first intended to secure rights for former slaves. It includes the Due Process and Equal Protection Clauses, among others. It was proposed on June 13, 1866, and was ratified on July 9, 1868. It is perhaps the most significant structural change to the Constitution since the passage of the United States Bill of Rights.
Justice	Justice concerns the proper ordering of things and persons within a society. As a concept it has been subject to philosophical, legal, and theological reflection and debate throughout history.
Earl Warren	Earl Warren was a California district attorney of Alameda County, the 20th Attorney General of California, the 30th Governor of California, and the 14th Chief Justice of the United States. As Chief Justice, his term of office was marked by numerous rulings affecting, among other things, the legal status of racial segregation, civil rights, separation of church and state, and police arrest procedure in the United States.
Civil Disobedience	Civil disobedience encompasses the active refusal to obey certain laws, demands and commands of a government or of an occupying power without resorting to physical violence.
De facto	De facto is a Latin expression that means "in fact" or "in practice" but not spelled out by law. The term de facto may also be used when there is no relevant law or standard, but a common practice is well established, although perhaps not quite universal. A de facto standard is a technical or other standard that is so dominant that everybody seems to follow it like an authorized standard.
De facto segregation	Segregation that is an unintended consequence of social or ecological arrangements is referred to as de facto segregation.
John F. Kennedy	John F. Kennedy was the thirty-fifth President of the United States, serving from 1961 until his assassination in 1963.
James Meredith	James Meredith is an American civil rights movement figure. He was the first African-American student at the University of Mississippi, an event that was a flash point in the American civil rights movement.
Christian	A Christian is a person who adheres to Christianity, a monotheistic religion centered on the

	life and teachings of Jesus Christ as presented in the New Testament and interpreted by Christians to have been prophesied in the Hebrew Bible/Old Testament.
Jail	Jail is a correctional institution used to detain persons who are in the lawful custody of the government. This includes either accused persons awaiting trial or for those who have been convicted of a crime and are serving a sentence of less than one year.
Lyndon Baines Johnson	Lyndon Baines Johnson was the thirty-sixth President of the United States, serving from 1963-1969. A Democrat, Johnson succeeded to the presidency following the assassination of President Kennedy, and after completing Kennedy's term was elected President in his own right in a landslide victory in the 1964 Presidential election.
Anthony Oberschall	Anthony Oberschall is Professor of Sociology at the University of North Carolina. He teaches international conflict management in a join t UNC-Duke University program on Peace and Conflict Resolution. He has researched and written about the break-up of Yugoslavia and post-war reconstruction.
Income	Income, generally defined, is the money that is received as a result of the normal business activities of an individual or a business.
Sears	Sears is an American mid-range chain of international department stores, founded by Richard Sears and Alvah Roebuck in the late 19th century. It operates in Canada under Sears Canada, Mexico under Sears Mexico and Guatemala under Homemart, S.A.
Expectation	Expectation is what is considered the most likely to happen.
Black Power	Black Power is a movement among Black people throughout the world, especially those in the United States. Most prominent in the late 1960s and early 1970s, the movement emphasized racial pride and the creation of black political and cultural institutions to nurture and promote black collective interests, advance black values, and secure black autonomy.
Stokely Carmichael	Stokely Carmichael was a Trinidadian-American black activist active in the 1960s American Civil Rights Movement. He rose to prominence first as a leader of the Student Nonviolent Coordinating Committee and later as the "Honorary Prime Minister" of the Black Panther Party.
Committee	A committee is a type of small deliberative assembly that is usually subordinate to another, larger deliberative assembly.
Power	Power is the ability of a person to control or influence the choices of other persons. The term authority is often used for power perceived as legitimate by the social structure. Power can be seen as evil or unjust; indeed all evil and injustice committed by man against man involve power.
Student	A student could be described as 'one who directs zeal at a subject'.
Black Panther party	The Black Panther Party was an African-American organization established to promote civil rights and self-defense. It was active in the United States from the mid-1960s into the 1970s.
Civil Disorder	Civil disorder is a broad term that is typically used by law enforcement to describe one or more forms of disturbance caused by a group of people.
Communist Party	Communist party is generally used to identify any political party which has adopted communist ideology. However, the Leninist concept of a communist party includes not only ideological orientation, but also a wide set of organizational policies. The communist party is, at least according to Leninist theory, the vanguard party of the working class.
Disorder	In medicine, a disorder is a functional abnormality or disturbance. In many cases, the terms "disorder", "disease" and "illness" are used interchangeably.[3] However, the term "disorder" is often considered more value-neutral than the term "disease", and is preferred by some

Go to **Cram101.com** for the Practice Tests for this Chapter.

	patients with these conditions.Medical disorders can be categorized into mental disorders or physical disorders. Mental disorder is the far more common term and physical disorder is mostly used just for distinction purposes.
Joyce Ladner	Joyce Ladner and her sister, Dorie, organized civil rights protests alongside Medgar Evers and other students from the Student Nonviolent Coordinating Committee. She was appointed assistant professor of sociology and curriculum specialist at the South Illinois University at East St. Louis.
Kerner Commission	The Kerner Commission was a 11-member commission was created by President Lyndon B. Johnson to investigate the causes of the 1967 race riots in the United States.
Peace	Peace is a state of harmony, the absence of hostility. This term is applied to describe a cessation of violent international conflict; in this international context, peace is the opposite of war. Peace can also describe a relationship between any parties characterized by respect, justice, and goodwill.
Peace and Freedom Party	The Peace and Freedom Party is a ballot-listed minor political party in California.
Bobby Seale	Bobby Seale is an American civil rights activist, who along with Dr. Huey P. Newton, co-founded the Black Panther Party For Self Defense in 1966.
Society	A society is a grouping of individuals, which is characterized by common interest and may have distinctive culture and institutions.
Jesse Jackson	Jesse Jackson is an American civil rights activist and Baptist minister. He was a candidate for the Democratic presidential nomination in 1984 and 1988 and served as "shadow senator" for the District of Columbia from 1991 to 1997. He was the founder of both entities that merged to form Rainbow/PUSH. Representative Jesse Jackson, Jr. is his eldest son.
Malcolm X	Malcolm X was an American Black Muslim minister and a spokesman for the Nation of Islam. After leaving the Nation of Islam in 1964, he made the pilgrimage, the Hajj, to Mecca and became a Sunni Muslim. He also founded the Muslim Mosque, Inc. and the Organization of Afro-American Unity. Less than a year later, he was assassinated in Washington Heights on the first day of National Brotherhood Week.
Mary Pattillo-McCoy	Mary Pattillo-McCoy is Professor of African American Studies and Chair & Professor of Sociology at Northwestern University. One of her best known books is Blakc Picket Fences: Privilege and Peril among the Black Middle Class. Her publication Black on the Block: The Politics of Race and Class in the City, is bases o five years of enthnographic data exploring the simultaneous in a black Chicago community.
Islam	Islam is a monotheistic religion originating with the teachings of Muhammad, a 7th-century Arab religious and political figure. Islam includes many religious practices. Adherents are generally required to observe the Five Pillars of Islam, which are five duties that unite Muslims into a community.
Muslim	A Muslim is an adherent of the religion of Islam. They believe that there is only one God, translated in Arabic as Allah. They also believe that Islam existed long before Muhammad and that the religion has evolved with time.
Nation of Islam	The original Nation of Islam was founded in Detroit, Michigan in 1930 by Wallace Fard Muhammad also known as Master W. D. Fard Muhammad. The Nation of Islam teaches that W. Fard Muhammad is both the "Messiah" of Christianity and the Mahdi of Islam. One of Fard's first disciples was Elijah Muhammad, who led the organization from 1935 through 1975.

Primetime	Primetime is a general-interest American news magazine show which debuted on ABC in 1989 with co-hosts Sam Donaldson and Diane Sawyer.
Lifestyle	In sociology a lifestyle is the way a person lives. This includes patterns of social relations, consumption, entertainment, and dress. A lifestyle typically also reflects an individual's attitudes, values or worldview.
African Americans	African Americans are citizens or residents of the United States whose ancestors, usually in predominant part, were indigenous to Sub-Saharan Africa. Most are the descendants of captive Africans who were enslaved within the boundaries of the present United States.
Head Start	Head Start is a program of the United States Department of Health and Human Services that focuses on assisting children from low-income families. Created in 1965, Head Start is the longest-running national school readiness program in the United States. It provides comprehensive education, health, nutrition, and parent involvement services to low-income children and their families.
Higher education	Higher education is education provided by universities, vocational universities and other collegial institutions that award academic degrees, such as career colleges. Higher education includes teaching, research and social services activities of universities, and within the realm of teaching, it includes both the undergraduate level and the graduate level.
Brown v. Board of Education	Brown v. Board of Education was a landmark decision of the United States Supreme Court, which overturned earlier rulings going back to Plessy v. Ferguson in 1896, by declaring that state laws which established separate public schools for black and white students denied black children equal educational opportunities.
Civil Rights	Civil rights are the protections and privileges of personal liberty given to all citizens by law. Civil rights are rights that are bestowed by nations on those within their territorial boundaries.
De facto	De facto is a Latin expression that means "in fact" or "in practice" but not spelled out by law. The term de facto may also be used when there is no relevant law or standard, but a common practice is well established, although perhaps not quite universal. A de facto standard is a technical or other standard that is so dominant that everybody seems to follow it like an authorized standard.
De facto segregation	Segregation that is an unintended consequence of social or ecological arrangements is referred to as de facto segregation.
Harvard University	Harvard University is a private university in Cambridge, Massachusetts, U.S., and a member of the Ivy League. Founded in 1636 by the colonial Massachusetts legislature, Harvard is the oldest institution of higher learning in the United States. It is also the first and oldest corporation in North America.
Gary Orfield	Gary Orfield is an American professor of education, law, political science and urban planning at UCLA. He s co-founder of The Civil Rights Project, to provide needed intellectual capital to academics, policy makers and civil rights advocates. His central interest is the development and implementation of social policy, with a central focus on the impact of policy on equal opportunity for success in American society.
Curriculum	In formal education, a curriculum is the set of courses, and their content, offered at a school or university.
Segregation	Segregation may be mandated by law or exist through social norms. Segregation may be maintained by means ranging from discrimination in hiring and in the rental and sale of housing to certain races to vigilante violence such as lynchings; a situation that arises when members of different races mutually prefer to associate and do business with members of their own race would usually be described as separation or de facto separation of the races

rather than segregation.

Maureen T. Hallinan	Maureen T. Hallinan is Professor of Sociology and director of the Center for Research on Educational Opportunity, Institute for Educational Initiatives at the University of Notre Dame. She was the principal investigator of the Comparative Analysis of Best Practices in Public and Private Elementary and Secondary Schools project.
Income	Income, generally defined, is the money that is received as a result of the normal business activities of an individual or a business.
Poverty	Poverty may be seen as the collective condition of poor people, or of poor groups, and in this sense entire nation-states are sometimes regarded as poor. Although the most severe poverty is in the developing world, there is evidence of poverty in every region.
Prosperity	Prosperity has come to mean an abundance of items of economic value, or the state of controlling or possessing such items, and encompasses money, real estate and personal property. In economics, refers to the value of assets owned minus the value of liabilities owed at a point in time.
Underemployment	A condition of having to work part-time when full-time work is desired and sought after is an underemployment.
Devah Pager	Devah Pager is Professor of Sociology at the Princeton University. Her research focuses on institutions affection racial stratification, including education, labor markets, and criminal justice system. She has research a seried of field experiments studying discrimination agains minorities and ex-offenders in the low-wage labor market.
Wage	A wage is a compensation workers receive in exchange for their labor.
City	A city is an urban area with a large population and a particular administrative, legal, or historical status.
Capitalism	Capitalism generally refers to an economic system in which the means of production are all or mostly privately owned and operated for profit, and in which investments, distribution, income, production and pricing of goods and services are determined through the operation of a free market.
Coalition	A coalition is an alliance among entities, during which they cooperate in joint action, each in their own self-interest. This alliance may be temporary or a matter of convenience. A coalition thus differs from a more formal covenant.
Louis Farrakhan	Louis Farrakhan is the Supreme Minister of the Nation of Islam as the National Representative of Elijah Muhammad. He is also well-known as an advocate for African American interests and a critic of American society. Farrakhan currently resides in Kenwood, an affluent neighborhood on the south side of Chicago, and part time at a Nation of Islam farm in New Buffalo, Michigan.
Hacker	In a security context, a hacker is someone involved in computer security/insecurity, specializing in the discovery of exploits in systems (for exploitation or prevention), or in obtaining or preventing unauthorized access to systems through skills, tactics and detailed knowledge.
Andrew Hacker	Andrew Hacker is an American political scientist and public intellectual. He is also Professor Emeritus in the Department of Political Science at Queens College in New York. He is working in a book on higher education in America in collaboration with Claudia Dreifus.
Islam	Islam is a monotheistic religion originating with the teachings of Muhammad, a 7th-century Arab religious and political figure. Islam includes many religious practices. Adherents are generally required to observe the Five Pillars of Islam, which are five duties that unite Muslims into a community.

Kinship	Kinship is the most basic principle of organizing individuals into social groups, roles, and categories. It was originally thought to be determined by biological descent, a view that was challenged by David M. Schneider in his work on Symbolic Kinship.
Million Man March	The Million Man March was a Black march convened by Nation of Islam leader Louis Farrakhan in Washington, DC on October 16, 1995. The event included efforts to register African Americans to vote in US Elections and increase black involvement in volunteerism and community activism.
Muslim	A Muslim is an adherent of the religion of Islam. They believe that there is only one God, translated in Arabic as Allah. They also believe that Islam existed long before Muhammad and that the religion has evolved with time.
Nation of Islam	The original Nation of Islam was founded in Detroit, Michigan in 1930 by Wallace Fard Muhammad also known as Master W. D. Fard Muhammad. The Nation of Islam teaches that W. Fard Muhammad is both the "Messiah" of Christianity and the Mahdi of Islam. One of Fard's first disciples was Elijah Muhammad, who led the organization from 1935 through 1975.
Single-parent	A Single-parent is a parent who cares for children without the assistance of another person in the home. The legal definition of "single parenthood" may vary according to the local laws of different nations or regions.
Tucker	Tucker was the leading proponent of American individualist anarchism in the 19th century. He defined 'socialism' in a very individualist manner contrary to collectivist socialists, since he supported individual ownership of property.
Lynne M. Casper	Lynne M. Casper is Professor of Sociology at the University of Southern California. She was also the Health Scientist Administrator and Demographer in the Demographic and Behavioral Sciences Branch at the National Institute of Child Health and Human Development. She is the author of The Interagency Forum on Child and Family Statistics.
Milton Gordon	Milton Gordon is an American sociologist. He is most noted for having devised a theory on the Seven Stages of Assimilation.
Alvin Gouldner	Alvin Gouldner was professor of sociology at Washington University in St. Louis. His early works such as Patterns in Industrial Bureaucracy can be seen as important as they worked within the existing fields of sociology but adopted the principles of a critical intellectual. He is probably most remembered for his work, The Coming Crisis of Western Sociology.
Middle class	A social class broadly defined occupationally as those working in white-collar and lower managerial occupations and is sometimes defined by reference to income levels or subjective identification of the participants in the study are referred to as middle class.
Daniel Patrick Moynihan	Daniel Patrick Moynihan was an American politician and sociologist. He was an Assistant Secretary of Labor for policy in the Kennedy Administration and in the early part of the Lyndon Johnson Administration. He coined the term "professionalization of reform" by which the government bureaucracy thinks up problems for government to solve rather than simply responding to problems identified elsewhere.
Negro	Negro is a term referring to people of Black African ancestry. Prior to the shift in the lexicon of American and worldwide classification of race and ethnicity in the late 1960s, the appellation was accepted as a normal neutral formal term both by those of Black African descent as well as non-African blacks.
Race	The term race refers to the concept of dividing people into populations or groups on the basis of various sets of characteristics and beliefs about common ancestry. The most widely used human racial categories are based on visible traits especially skin color, facial features and hair texture, and self-identification.

107

Max weber	Max Weber was a German political economist and sociologist who is considered one of the founders of the modern study of sociology and public administration. His major works deal with rationalisation in sociology of religion and government, but he also contributed much in the field of economics. His most famous work is his essay The Protestant Ethic and the Spirit of Capitalism, which began his work in the sociology of religion.
Charles Willie	Charles Willie is the Charles William Eliot Professor of Education, Emeritus at Harvard University. He is a sociologist whose areas of research include desegregation, higher education, public health, race relations, urban community problems, and family life. He is a member of Alpha Phi Alpha, the first intercollegiate Greek-letter fraternity established for African Americans.
William Julius Wilson	William Julius Wilson is an American sociologist. In The Declining Significance of Race: Blacks and Changing American Institutions he argues that the significance of race is waning, and an African-American's class is comparatively more important in determining his or her life chances.
Patricia J. Williams	Patricia J. Williams is a prominent law critic and a proponent of critical race theory, an offshoot of 1960s social movements that emphasizes race as a fundamental determinant of the American legal system. She also worked as a consumer advocate in the office of the City Attorney in Los Angeles.
Discrimination	Discrimination refers to the denial of equal access to social resources to people on the basis of their group membership.
Fair Housing	In the United States, the fair housing policies date largely from the 1960s. Originally, the terms fair housing and open housing came from a political movement of the time to outlaw discrimination in the rental or purchase of homes and a broad range of other housing-related transactions, such as advertising, mortgage lending, homeowner's insurance and zoning. Later, the same language was used in laws.
Civil Rights Act of 1968	On April 11, 1968, President Lyndon Johnson signed the Civil Rights Act of 1968, which was meant as a follow-up to the Civil Rights Act of 1964. While the Civil Rights Act of 1866 prohibited discrimination in housing, there were no federal enforcement provisions. The 1968 act expanded on previous acts and prohibited discrimination concerning the sale, rental, and financing of housing based on race, religion, national origin, and as of 1974, sex; as of 1988, the act protects the handicapped and families with children.
John F. Kennedy	John F. Kennedy was the thirty-fifth President of the United States, serving from 1961 until his assassination in 1963.
Redlining	Redlining is the practice of denying or increasing the cost of services, such as banking, insurance, access to jobs, access to health care, or even supermarkets to residents in certain, often racially determined, areas. The most devastating form of redlining, and the most common use of the term, refers to mortgage discrimination, in which middle-income black and Hispanic residents are denied loans that are made available to lower-income whites.
Market	A market is a social arrangement that allows buyers and sellers to discover information and carry out a voluntary exchange of goods or services. It is one of the two key institutions that organize trade, along with the right to own property.
Arrest	An arrest is the act of depriving a person of his or her liberty usually in relation to the investigation and prevention of crime. The term is Norman in origin and is related to the French word arrêt, meaning "stop".
Crime	A normative definition views crime as deviant behavior that violates prevailing norms, specifically, cultural standards prescribing how humans ought to behave.
Criminal justice	Criminal justice is the system of legislation, practices, and organizations, used by

Go to **Cram101.com** for the Practice Tests for this Chapter.

	government or the state, which are all directed to maintain social control, deter and control crime, and sanctioning those who violate laws.
Proposition	In philosophy and logic, proposition refers to either the content or meaning of a meaningful declarative sentence or the string of symbols, marks, or sounds that make up a meaningful declarative sentence. Propositions in either case are intended to be truth-bearers, that is, they are either true or false.
Violence	Violence is, on the one hand, acts of aggression and abuse that cause' or intend to cause injury to person or persons. Central to this concept of violence is the presence of the definite intention to cause significant injury, damage and harm.
Justice	Justice concerns the proper ordering of things and persons within a society. As a concept it has been subject to philosophical, legal, and theological reflection and debate throughout history.
Police	Police are agents or agencies empowered to effect public and social order through various means of coercion including the legitimate use of force.
Police officer	A police officer is a warranted employee of a police force. Among the responsibilities of a police officer are to maintain public order, prevent and detect crime and apprehend offenders, using force when necessary.
Death penalty	Death penalty is the execution of a convicted criminal by the state as punishment for crimes known as capital crimes or capital offences. The execution of criminals and political opponents was used by nearly all societies—both to punish crime and to suppress political dissent.
Victimology	Victimology is the study of why certain people are victims of crime and how lifestyles affect the chances that a certain person will fall victim to a crime. The field can cover a wide number of disciplines, including sociology, psychology, criminal justice, law and advocacy.
Victimization surveys	Victimization surveys attempts to bypass the underreporting problem by going directly to the victims. The National Crime Victimization Survey (NCVS) is conducted by the U.S. Bureau of the Census in cooperation with the Bureau of Justice Statistics and the U.S. Department of Justice. The NCVS polls over 50,000 households, totaling over 100,000 individuals, in the United States annually using a multistage sample of housing units. Individuals over 12 years old in selected households are interviewed every six months for about three years.
Health care	Health care is the prevention, treatment, and management of illness and the preservation of mental and physical well being through the services offered by the medical, nursing, and allied health professions. In most developed countries and many developing countries health care is provided to everyone regardless of their ability to pay. The health care industry is one of the world's largest and fastest-growing industries.
Raquel Pinderhughes	Raquel Pinderhughes is Professor of Urban Studies at San Francisco State University. Her teaching and research focus on improving quality of life for people living and working in cities. Her book, Alternative Urban Futures: Planning for Sustainable Development in Cities throughout the World focuses on planning and policy approaches and appropriate technologies that can be used to minimize a city's impact on the environment while providing urban residents with the infrastructure and services they need to sustain a high quality of urban life.
Howard Waitzkin	Howard Waitzkin is Professor of Sociology at the University of New Mexico. His work has focused on health policy in comparative international perspective and on psychosocial issues in primary care. He co-authored the proposal for a single-payer national health program that was published in the New England Journal of Medicine.
Mortality	Mortality rate is a measure of the number of deaths in some population, scaled to the size of

	that population, per unit time. Mortality rate is typically expressed in units of deaths per 1000 individuals per year; thus, a mortality rate of 9.5 in a population of 100,000 would mean 950 deaths per year in that entire population. It is distinct from morbidity rate, which refers to the number of individuals who have contracted a disease during a given time period or the number who currently have that disease, scaled to the size of the population.
Mortality rate	Mortality rate is a measure of the number of deaths in some population, scaled to the size of that population, per unit time. Mortality rate is typically expressed in units of deaths per 1000 individuals per year; thus, a mortality rate of 10000.5 in a population of 100,000 would mean 1,000,500 deaths per year in the entire population.
Reconstruction	Reconstruction was the attempt from 1865 to 1877 in U.S. history to resolve the issues of the American Civil War, when both the Confederacy and slavery were destroyed. Reconstruction addressed the return to the Union of the secessionist Southern states, the status of the leaders of the Confederacy, and the Constitutional and legal status of the Negro Freedmen.
Politics	Politics is the process by which groups of people make decisions. Although the term is generally applied to behavior within governments, politics is observed in all human group interactions, including corporate, academic, and religious institutions.
George W. Bush	George W. Bush is the forty-third and current President of the United States of America. Originally inaugurated on January 20, 2001, Bush was elected president in the 2000 presidential election and re-elected in the 2004 presidential election. He previously served as the forty-sixth Governor of Texas from 1995 to 2000.
Gerrymandering	Gerrymandering is a form of redistricting in which electoral district or constituency boundaries are manipulated for an electoral advantage. Gerrymandering may be used to advantage or disadvantage particular constituents, such as members of a racial, linguistic, religious or class group, often in the favor of ruling incumbents or a specific political party.
Al Gore	Al Gore is an American environmental activist, author, businessperson, and former politician.
Tracking	Tracking is the practice, in education, of placing students into different groups within a school, based on academic abilities. For years, schools in the United States and Great Britain have used tracking as a way of dividing students into different "tracks" to facilitate learning. Though the terms "tracking" and "ability grouping" are often used interchangeably, Gamoran 1992 differentiates between the two. He uses the term "tracking" to describe the manner by which students are separated into groups for all academic subjects, but "ability grouping," on the other hand, is the within-class separation of students into groups, based on academic ability. High ability groups are often assigned special work that is more advanced than that of the other students in the class.
Student	A student could be described as 'one who directs zeal at a subject'.
Voting	Voting is a method of decision making wherein a group such as a meeting or an electorate attempts to gauge its opinion—usually as a final step following discussions or debates.
Assimilation	A minority group's internalization of the values and norms of the dominant culture is referred to as assimilation.
Civil Rights Movement	Historically, the civil rights movement was a concentrated period of time around the world of approximately one generation (1954-1980) wherein there was much worldwide civil unrest and popular rebellion.

Go to **Cram101.com** for the Practice Tests for this Chapter.

Hispanic	Hispanic is a term that historically denoted relation to the ancient Hispania and its peoples. The term now refers to the culture and people of the Spanish-speaking countries of Hispanic America and Spain; or countries with a historical legacy from Spain, including the
Hispanic American	Hispanic American is an American citizen or resident of Hispanic ethnicity and can identify themselves as having Hispanic Cultural heritage. According to the 2000 Census, Hispanics constitute the second largest ethnic group in the United States, compromizing roughly 12.5% of the population.
Population	A population is the collection of people or organisms of a particular species living in a given geographic area or space, usually measured by a census.
Latino	Latino is a term that is historically denoted relation to the ancient Latina tribe, who were an ancient Italic people who migrated to central Italy. Since its official adoption, the definition and usage of the term by the Federal Government is strictly as an ethnic, as opposed to racial, identifier, used together with the term Hispanic.
Identity	Identity is an umbrella term used throughout the social sciences to describe an individual's comprehension of him or herself as a discrete, separate entity.
Immigration	Although human migration has existed for hundreds of thousands of years, immigration in the modern sense refers to movement of people from one nation-state to another, where they are not citizens.
Language	A language is a system of symbols and the rules used to manipulate them. Language can also refer to the use of such systems as a general phenomenon. Because a language also has a grammar, it can manipulate its symbols to express clear and regular relationships between them.
Bilingual	Bilingual model In this model, native language and the community language are simultaneously taught. The advantage is literacy in two languages as the outcome. However, teacher training must be high in both languages and in techniques for teaching a second language.
Bilingual Education	An educational approach whose aim is to teach academic subjects to immigrant children in their native languages while gradually adding English instruction is referred to a bilingual education.
Independent	The independent variables are those that are deliberately manipulated to invoke a change in the dependent variables. In short, "if x is given, then y occurs", where x represents the independent variables and y represents the dependent variables.
Private school	Private school is a school not administered by local, state, or national government, which retain the right to select their student body and are funded in whole or in part by charging their students tuition. It is a range from pre-school to tertiary level institutions. Annual tuitions at K-12 schools range from nothing at tuition-free schools to more than $40,000 at several boarding schools.
Treaty of Guadalupe Hidalgo	The Treaty of Guadalupe Hidalgo is the peace treaty, largely dictated by the United States to the interim government of a militarily occupied Mexico, that ended the Mexican-American War.
Politics	Politics is the process by which groups of people make decisions. Although the term is generally applied to behavior within governments, politics is observed in all human group interactions, including corporate, academic, and religious institutions.
George W. Bush	George W. Bush is the forty-third and current President of the United States of America. Originally inaugurated on January 20, 2001, Bush was elected president in the 2000 presidential election and re-elected in the 2004 presidential election. He previously served as the forty-sixth Governor of Texas from 1995 to 2000.

Al Gore	Al Gore is an American environmental activist, author, businessperson, and former politician.
Maquiladora	A maquiladora is a factory that imports materials and equipment on a duty-free and tariff-free basis for assembly or manufacturing and then re-exports the assembled product, usually back to the originating country.
Jimmy Carter	Jimmy Carter was the thirty-ninth President of the United States from 1977 to 1981, and the Nobel Peace laureate of 2002. Prior to becoming president, Carter served two terms in the Georgia Senate, and was the 76th Governor of Georgia from 1971 to 1975.
Castro, Fidel	Castro, Fidel is the current President of Cuba, though currently with his duties transferred. He became First Secretary of the Communist Party of Cuba, and led the transformation of Cuba into a one-party socialist republic. He gained an ardent, but limited, following and also drew the attention of the authorities.
Cuban American	Cuban American is a United States citizen whose trace their ancestry to Cuba. Many communities throughout the United States have significant Cuban American populations. It represent a total of only 4% of the Hispanic population in the United States. However, Miami, Florida stands out as the most prominent Cuban American community.
Marielita	Marielita is a term applied to roughly 125,000 people who fled to the United States from the Cuban port of Mariel as part of the exodus of refugees in 1980.
Status	In sociology or anthropology, social status is the honor or prestige attached to one's position in society one's social position. The stratification system, which is the system of distributing rewards to the members of society, determines social status. Social status, the position or rank of a person or group within the stratification system, can be determined two ways. One can earn their social status by their own achievements, which is known as achieved status, or one can be placed in the stratification system by their inherited position, which is called ascribed status.
Anglo	The term Anglo is used as a prefix to indicate a relation to the Angles, England or the English people, as in the phrases 'Anglo-Saxon', 'Anglo-American', 'Anglo-Celtic', and 'Anglo-Indian'. It is often used alone, somewhat loosely, to refer to a person or people of English ethnicity in the The Americas, Australia and Southern Africa. It is also used, both in English-speaking and non-English-speaking countries, to refer to Anglophone people of other European origins.
Little Havana	Little Havana is a neighborhood in the city of Miami, with many Cuban immigrant residents.
National Science Foundation	The National Science Foundation is a United States government agency that supports fundamental research and education in all the non-medical fields of science and engineering. With an annual budget of about $5.91 billion as of fiscal year 2007, it funds approximately 20 percent of all federally supported basic research conducted by the United States' colleges and universities. In some fields, such as mathematics, computer science, economics and the social sciences, this foundation is the major source of federal backing.
Culture	Culture generally refers to patterns of human activity and the symbolic structures that give such activity significant importance. Culture has been called "the way of life for an entire society." As such, it includes codes of manners, dress, language, religion, rituals, norms of behavior such as law and morality, and systems of belief.
Gay	Gay usually describes a person's sexual orientation, being the standard term for homosexual. Gay sometimes also refers to commonalities shared by homosexual people, as in "gay history", the ideological concept of a hypothetical gay culture, as in "gay music." The word gay is sometimes used to refer to same-sex relationships.
Homosexuality	Homosexuality can refer to both attraction or sexual behavior between people of the same sex, or to a sexual orientation. When describing the latter, it refers to enduring sexual and

	romantic attraction towards those of the same sex, but not necessarily to sexual behavior.
Lesbian	A lesbian is a woman who is romantically and sexually attracted only to other women. Some women in same-sex relationships do not identify as lesbian, but as bisexual, queer, or another label. As with any interpersonal activity, sexual expression depends on the context of the relationship.
South America	South America is a continent occupying the southern part of the supercontinent of America. It sits entirely in the Western Hemisphere, and mostly in the Southern Hemisphere with a small portion in the Northern Hemisphere. It is bordered on the west by the Pacific Ocean and on the north and east by the Atlantic Ocean. North America and the Caribbean Sea lie to the northwest.
Unemployment	Unemployment is the condition of willing workers lacking jobs or "gainful employment". A key measure is the unemployment rate, which is the number of unemployed workers divided by the total civilian labor force.

Aztec	Aztec is a term used to refer to certain ethnic groups of central Mexico, particularly those groups who spoke the Nahuatl language and who achieved political and military dominance over large parts of Mesoamerica in the 14th, 15th and 16th centuries, a period referred to as the
Hispanic	Hispanic is a term that historically denoted relation to the ancient Hispania and its peoples. The term now refers to the culture and people of the Spanish-speaking countries of Hispanic America and Spain; or countries with a historical legacy from Spain, including the Southwestern United States and Florida; the African nations of Equatorial Guinea, Western Sahara and the Northern coastal region of Morocco; the Asia-Pacific nations of the
Hispanic American	Hispanic American is an American citizen or resident of Hispanic ethnicity and can identify themselves as having Hispanic Cultural heritage. According to the 2000 Census, Hispanics constitute the second largest ethnic group in the United States, compromizing roughly 12.5% of the population.
Maya civilization	The Maya civilization is a Mesoamerican civilization, noted for the only known fully developed written language of the pre-Columbian Americas, as well as its spectacular art, monumental architecture, and sophisticated mathematical and astronomical systems.
Mexican Americans	Mexican Americans are citizens of the United States of Mexican ancestry. Mexican Americans account for 9% of the country's population. Mexican Americans form the largest White Hispanic group in the United States. Mexican Americans trace their ancestry to Mexico and Mesoamerica, a country located in North America; the Southwest United States; bounded on the north by the United States; and many different European countries, especially Spain.
Mexican-American War	The Mexican-American War was an armed military conflict between the United States and Mexico in the wake of the U.S. annexation of Texas. The most important consequence of the war for the United States was the Mexican Cession, in which the Mexican territories of Alta California and Santa Fé de Nuevo México were ceded to the United States under the terms of the Treaty of Guadalupe Hidalgo. In Mexico, the enormous loss of territory following the war encouraged its government to enact policies to colonize its northern territories as a hedge against further losses.
Puerto Rican	A Puerto Rican is a citizen who was raised in the eastern United States territory of Puerto Rico. A Puerto Rican, who also commonly identify themselves as Boricua, are largely the descendants of native Taíno Indians, Europeans, African slaves or a blend of these groups which has produced a very multi-cultural and diversified population. The population is estimated to be between 8 to 10 million worldwide.
Treaty of Guadalupe Hidalgo	The Treaty of Guadalupe Hidalgo is the peace treaty, largely dictated by the United States to the interim government of a militarily occupied Mexico, that ended the Mexican-American War.
Citizenship	Citizenship is membership in a society, community, or and carries with it rights to political participation; a person having such membership is a citizen.
Civilization	Civilization is a kind of human society or culture; specifically, a civilization is usually understood to be a complex society characterized by the practice of agriculture and settlement in cities. Civilization can also refer to society as a whole. To nineteenth-century English anthropologist Edward Burnett Tylor, for example, civilization was "the total social heredity of mankind."
Controversy	A controversy is a matter of opinion over which parties actively disagree, argue, or debate. Controversies can range in size from private disputes between two individuals to large-scale disagreements between societies.
Immigration	Although human migration has existed for hundreds of thousands of years, immigration in the modern sense refers to movement of people from one nation-state to another, where they are

Go to **Cram101.com** for the Practice Tests for this Chapter.

	not citizens.
Ernesto Galarza	Ernesto Galarza was a labor organizer, historian, professor, and community activist. He researched the condition of the braceros, the Mexican contract workers in the California agricultural industry. This led him to write his most significant book, Merchants of Labor, an expose of the exploitation of braceros.
Mexican Revolution	The Mexican Revolution was a major armed struggle that started with an uprising led by Francisco I. Madero against longtime dictator Porfirio Díaz. The first of the major revolutions of the 20th century, the Mexican Revolution was characterized by several socialist, liberal, anarchist, populist, and agrarianist movements.
La Raza	La Raza is sometimes used to denote people of the Latino and Chicano world, as well by Mestizos who share the pride of their Native American or national Hispanic heritage. Nonetheless, the term and idea associated with it have been mainly adopted by some Mexican people in the United States to express pride in their nation.
Mojados	Mojados is a municipality located in the province of Valladolid, Castile and León, Spain.
Wetback	Wetback is a derogatory term for a person that has immigrated illegally to the United States.
Civil Rights	Civil rights are the protections and privileges of personal liberty given to all citizens by law. Civil rights are rights that are bestowed by nations on those within their territorial boundaries.
Culture	Culture generally refers to patterns of human activity and the symbolic structures that give such activity significant importance. Culture has been called "the way of life for an entire society." As such, it includes codes of manners, dress, language, religion, rituals, norms of behavior such as law and morality, and systems of belief.
Culture of poverty	The culture of poverty concept is a social theory explaining the cycle of poverty. Based on the concept that the poor have a unique value system, the culture of poverty theory suggests the poor remain in poverty because of their adaptations to the burdens of poverty.
Culture-of-poverty theory	Culture-of-poverty theory is a social theory explaining the cycle of poverty. Based on the concept that the poor have a unique value system, it suggests the poor remain in poverty because of their adaptations to the burdens of poverty.
Oscar Lewis	Oscar Lewis was an American anthropologist. He introduced the concept of culture of poverty. He was also key in starting the Department of Anthroplogy at the University of Illinois and served as U.S. Representative of the Inter-American Indian Institute in Mexico to work on rural developments.
Poverty	Poverty may be seen as the collective condition of poor people, or of poor groups, and in this sense entire nation-states are sometimes regarded as poor. Although the most severe poverty is in the developing world, there is evidence of poverty in every region.
Chicano	Chicano is a cultural identity used primarily by people of Mexican descent in the United States. While its meaning has changed over time and varies regionally, it tends to refer to a Mexican American (usually second- or third-generation) who has a strong sense of ethnic identity and an accompanying political consciousness.
Herbert J. Gans	Herbert J. Gans is an American sociologist. One of the most prolific and influential sociologists of his generation, Gans trained in urban planning at the University of Pennsylvania, where he studied with Martin Meyerson and Lewis Mumford, among others. Gans made his reputation as a critic of urban renewal in the early 1960s. His study, The Urban Villagers focused on Boston's diverse West End neighborhood which was demolished for the construction of high rise apartments. Gans contrasted the diverse, lively community of immigrants and their children with the impersonal life in the modernist towers that replaced

them.

Raquel Pinderhughes	Raquel Pinderhughes is Professor of Urban Studies at San Francisco State University. Her teaching and research focus on improving quality of life for people living and working in cities. Her book, Alternative Urban Futures: Planning for Sustainable Development in Cities throughout the World focuses on planning and policy approaches and appropriate technologies that can be used to minimize a city's impact on the environment while providing urban residents with the infrastructure and services they need to sustain a high quality of urban life.
Underclass	A class of individuals in mature industrial societies situated at the bottom of the class system who have been systematically excluded from participation in economic life are the underclass.
United Farm Workers	The United Farm Workers is a labor union that evolved from unions founded in 1962 by César Chávez, Philip Vera Cruz, Dolores Huerta, and Larry Itliong. This union changed from a workers' rights organization that helped workers get unemployment insurance to that of a union of farmworkers almost overnight, when the National Farm Workers Association went out on strike in support of the mostly Filipino farmworkers of the Agricultural Workers Organizing Committee led by Larry Itliong in Delano, California who had previously initiated a grape strike on September 8, 1965. The NFWA and the AWOC, recognizing their common goals and methods, and realizing the strengths of coalition formation, jointly formed the United Farm Workers Organizing Committee on August 22, 1966. This organization eventually became the
Boycott	A boycott is the act of voluntarily abstaining from using, buying, or dealing with someone or some other organization as an expression of protest.
Politics	Politics is the process by which groups of people make decisions. Although the term is generally applied to behavior within governments, politics is observed in all human group interactions, including corporate, academic, and religious institutions.
Mario Barrera	Mario Barrera is Professor Emeritus of Chicano Studies at the University of California, Berkeley. His research interest include ethnicity theory, film, politics and ethnicity. He is the co-producer of the film Chicano Park and director and producer of Latino Stories of World War II.
Chicanismo	Chicanismo is a cultural movement begun in the 1930s in the Southwestern United States by Mexican Americans to recapture their Mexican, Native American culture.
Alianza Federal de Mercedes	Alianza Federal de Mercedes, which in English translates to Federal Land Grant Alliance, was a group led by Reies Tijerina based in New Mexico in the 1960s that fought for the land rights of Hispanic New Mexicans.
Carson National Forest	Carson National Forest is a national forest in northern New Mexico, United States.
Puerto Rico	Puerto Rico has had a per capita Gross Domestic Product estimate of $22,058, which demonstrates a growth over the $14,412 level. It also has a 48.2% poverty rate. Emigration has been a major part in Puerto Rico and hasgreatly lowered birth rate, suggests that the population will age rapidly and start to decline sometime within the next couple of decades.
Spanish American War	The Spanish American War was an armed military conflict between Spain and the United States that took place from April to August 1898. The war began due to American demands that Spain peacefully resolve the Cuban fight for independence, though strong expansionist sentiment in the United States may have also motivated the government to target Spain's other remaining overseas territories: Puerto Rico, the Philippines, Guam and the Caroline Islands.
City	A city is an urban area with a large population and a particular administrative, legal, or historical status.

New York	New York is a state in the Mid-Atlantic and Northeastern regions of the United States of America. With 62 counties, it is the country's third most populous state. It is bordered by Vermont, Massachusetts, Connecticut, New Jersey, and Pennsylvania, and shares a water border with Rhode Island as well as an international border with the Canadian provinces of Quebec and Ontario. Its five largest cities are New York City, Buffalo, Rochester, Yonkers, and Syracuse.
New York City	New York City two key demographic features are its population density and cultural diversity. It is exceptionally diverse. Throughout its history the city has been a major point of entry for immigrants; the term "melting pot" was first coined to describe densely populated immigrant neighborhoods on the Lower East Side. Violent crime in New York city has decreased 75% in the last twelve years and the murder rate.
Columbus, Christopher	Columbus, Christopher was a navigator, colonizer and one of the first Europeans to explore the Americas after the Vikings. Though not the first to reach the Americas from Europe, it was his voyages that led to general European awareness of the hemisphere and the successful establishment of European cultures in the New World.
Population	A population is the collection of people or organisms of a particular species living in a given geographic area or space, usually measured by a census.
Neocolonialism	Neocolonialism is a term used by some intellectuals to describe international economic arrangements by which former colonial powers maintained control of their former colonies and new dependencies following World War II.
Armed Forces	The armed forces of a state are its government-sponsored defence, fighting forces, and organizations.
Liberation	Liberation is based on the word liberty, related to the word liberal, and it is often understood as "to be freed from not having freedom to having freedom".
Status	In sociology or anthropology, social status is the honor or prestige attached to one's position in society one's social position. The stratification system, which is the system of distributing rewards to the members of society, determines social status. Social status, the position or rank of a person or group within the stratification system, can be determined two ways. One can earn their social status by their own achievements, which is known as achieved status, or one can be placed in the stratification system by their inherited position, which is called ascribed status.
Race	The term race refers to the concept of dividing people into populations or groups on the basis of various sets of characteristics and beliefs about common ancestry. The most widely used human racial categories are based on visible traits especially skin color, facial features and hair texture, and self-identification.
Social construction	A social construction is an institutionalized entity or artifact in a social system 'invented' or 'constructed' by participants in a particular culture or society that exists solely because people agree to behave as if it exists, or agree to follow certain conventional rules.
Drug	A drug is any chemical or biological substance, synthetic or non-synthetic, that when taken into the organism's body, will in some way alter the functions of that organism. This broad definition can be taken to include such substances as food.
Drug trade	The drug trade is a global black market consisting of the cultivation, manufacture, distribution and sale of illegal drugs. While some drugs are legal to possess and sell, in most jurisdictions laws prohibit the trade of certain types of drug.
Economics	Economics is the social science that studies the production, distribution, and consumption of goods and services. One of the uses of economics is to explain how economies work and what

	the relations are between economic players in the larger society.
Economy	An economy is the system of human activities related to the production, distribution, exchange, and consumption of goods and services of a country or other area. The composition of a given economy is inseparable from technological evolution, civilization's history and social organization.
Trafficking	Trafficking is the illegal transport, in particular, across a border. Taxes are avoided; or the goods themselves are illegal for unlicensed possession; or people are transported to a place where they are not allowed to be.
Free Trade	Free trade is a market model in which trade in goods and services between or within countries flow unhindered by government-imposed restrictions. Restrictions to trade include taxes and other legislation, such as tariff and non-tariff trade barriers.
North American Free Trade Agreement	The North American Free Trade Agreement is the trade bloc in North America along with its two supplements, the North American Agreement on Environmental Cooperation and The North American Agreement on Labor Cooperation, whose members are Canada, Mexico and the United States.
Gary Orfield	Gary Orfield is an American professor of education, law, political science and urban planning at UCLA. He s co-founder of The Civil Rights Project, to provide needed intellectual capital to academics, policy makers and civil rights advocates. His central interest is the development and implementation of social policy, with a central focus on the impact of policy on equal opportunity for success in American society.
Student	A student could be described as 'one who directs zeal at a subject'.
Compadrazgo	Compadrazgo is a form of fictive kinship found in Latin American culture, meaning literally co-parents but referring to co-godparenthood or joint sponsorship of a godchild or ritual object.
Family of Love	The Family of Love were a mystic religious sect known as the Familia Caritatis, founded by Hendrik Niclaes.
Life chances	Life chances are the opportunities each individual has to improve their quality of life. The concept was introduced by German sociologist Max Weber. It is a probabilistic concept, describing how likely it is, given certain factors, that an individual's life will turn out a certain way.
Mills	Mills is best remembered for studying the structure of Power in the U.S. in his book, The Power Elite. Mills was concerned with the responsibilities of intellectuals in post-World War II society, and advocated relevance and engagement over disinterested academic observation, as a "public intelligence apparatus" in challenging the crackpot policies of these institutional elite in the "Big Three", the economic, political and military.
Health care	Health care is the prevention, treatment, and management of illness and the preservation of mental and physical well being through the services offered by the medical, nursing, and allied health professions. In most developed countries and many developing countries health care is provided to everyone regardless of their ability to pay. The health care industry is one of the world's largest and fastest-growing industries.
Curanderismo	Curanderismo is a holistic system of Latin American folk medicine. It blends religious beliefs, faith, and prayer eith the use of herbs, massage, and other traditional methods of healing. It is used to treat ailments arising from physical, psychological, spiritual, or social conditions.
Catholicism	Catholicism is a denomination of Christianity whose center is the Vatican in Rome, Italy and dates from the original church created by the Apostle Peter, a disciple of Jesus Christ.
Susto	Susto is a cultural illness, specifically a "fright sickness" with strong psychological

Go to **Cram101.com** for the Practice Tests for this Chapter.

129

overtones.

Religion	A religion is a set of common beliefs and practices generally held by a group of people, often codified as prayer, ritual, and religious law. Religion also encompasses ancestral or cultural traditions, writings, history, and mythology, as well as personal faith and mystic experience.
El Dia de Los Muertos	El Dia de Los Muertos is a holiday celebrated mainly in Mexico and by people of Mexican heritage living in the United States and Canada. The holiday focuses on gatherings of family and friends to pray for and remember friends and relatives who have died. The celebration occurs on the 1st and 2nd of November, in connection with the Catholic holy days of All Saints' Day and All Souls' Day. Traditions include building private altars honoring the deceased, and using sugar skulls, marigolds, and the favorite foods and beverages of the departed.
Pentecostals	The majority believe that one must be saved by believing in Jesus as Lord and Savior for the forgiveness of sins and to be made acceptable to God. Pentecostals also typically believe, like most other evangelicals, that the Bible has definitive authority in matters of faith. Typically, Pentecostals that do not believe speaking in tongues is necessary for salvation-- the vast majority-- are from Trinitarian traditions.

Go to **Cram101.com** for the Practice Tests for this Chapter.

Arab	An Arab is a member of a complexly defined ethnic group who identifies as such on the basis of one or more of either genealogical, political, or linguistic grounds. The definition of an Arab is heavily disputed. It is usually defined independent of religious identity.
Arab Americans	Arab Americans are Americans of Arab ancestry and constitute an ethnicity made up of several waves of immigrants from twenty-two Arab countries, stretching from Morocco in the west to Oman in the south east to Iraq in the north. Although a highly diverse ethnic group, Arab Americans descend from a heritage that represents common linguistic, cultural, and political traditions.
Muslim	A Muslim is an adherent of the religion of Islam. They believe that there is only one God, translated in Arabic as Allah. They also believe that Islam existed long before Muhammad and that the religion has evolved with time.
Orientalism	Orientalism refers to the imitation or depiction of aspects of Eastern cultures in the West by writers, designers and artists, and can also refer to a sympathetic stance towards the region by a writer or other person.
Census	A census is the process of obtaining information about every member of a population. It can be contrasted with sampling in which information is only obtained from a subset of a population. As such it is a method used for accumulating statistical data, and it is also vital to democracy.
Ethnic identity	Ethnic identity refers to an enduring, basic aspect of the self that includes a sense of membership in an ethnic group and the attitudes and feelings related to that membership. Ethnic identity can vary with changes in social context.
Identity	Identity is an umbrella term used throughout the social sciences to describe an individual's comprehension of him or herself as a discrete, separate entity.
Population	A population is the collection of people or organisms of a particular species living in a given geographic area or space, usually measured by a census.
Hajj	The Hajj is a pilgrimage to Mecca. It is the largest annual pilgrimage in the world. It is the fifth pillar of Islam, an obligation that must be carried out at least once in their lifetime by every able-bodied Muslim who can afford to do so. It is a demonstration of the solidarity of the Muslim people, and their submission to the Arabic god Allah.
Shiite	Shiite is the largest minority denomination based on the Islamic faith after Sunni Islam. Shiite believe that the descendants from Muhammad through his beloved daughter Fatima Zahra and his son-in-law were the best source of knowledge about the Qur'an and Islam, the most trusted carriers and protectors of Muhammad's Sunnah, and the most worthy of emulation.
Sunni Muslims	Sunni Muslims are the largest denomination of Islam. They represent the branch of Islam that accepted the caliphate of Abu Bakr due to him being chosen by Shurah.
Jihad	Jihad is a religious duty of Muslims. In Arabic, Jihad means "strive" or "struggle". According to scholar John Esposito, Jihad requires Muslims to "struggle in the way of God" or "to struggle to improve one's self and/or society."
Geneive Abdo	Geneive Abdo is an author and analyst, who is the Liaison for the United Nation's Alliance of Civilizations, a project created to improve relations between Western and Islamic societies. Among her publications, there is a book name Mecca and Main Street: Muslim Life in America After 9/11.
Islam	Islam is a monotheistic religion originating with the teachings of Muhammad, a 7th-century Arab religious and political figure. Islam includes many religious practices. Adherents are generally required to observe the Five Pillars of Islam, which are five duties that unite Muslims into a community.

Nation of Islam	The original Nation of Islam was founded in Detroit, Michigan in 1930 by Wallace Fard Muhammad also known as Master W. D. Fard Muhammad. The Nation of Islam teaches that W. Fard Muhammad is both the "Messiah" of Christianity and the Mahdi of Islam. One of Fard's first disciples was Elijah Muhammad, who led the organization from 1935 through 1975.
Black Muslims	The term Black Muslim is widely credited to C. Eric Lincoln's 1961 book, The Black Muslims In America, which analyzed the growing influence of the Nation of Islam in the United States of America. The phrase is often used in the United States to denote members of Louis Farrakhan's separatist Black nationalist movement, the Nation of Islam. The Nation of Islam never appreciated being labeled "Black Muslims" and years afterward publicly denounced the title but as Malcolm X stated, "the name stuck." Today, the vast majority of Muslims in the African Diaspora are not members of the Nation of Islam. Rather, they follow local religious
Autobiography	An autobiography is a biography written by the subject or composed conjointly with a collaborative writer.
Martin Luther King, Jr.	Martin Luther King, Jr. was a leader in the American civil rights movement. King was a Baptist minister, one of the few leadership roles available to black men at the time. He became a civil rights activist early in his career. He led the Montgomery Bus Boycott and helped found the Southern Christian Leadership Conference, serving as its first president. His efforts led to the 1963 March on Washington, where King delivered his "I Have a Dream" speech. There, he raised public consciousness of the civil rights movement and established himself as one of the greatest orators in U.S. history.
Malcolm X	Malcolm X was an American Black Muslim minister and a spokesman for the Nation of Islam. After leaving the Nation of Islam in 1964, he made the pilgrimage, the Hajj, to Mecca and became a Sunni Muslim. He also founded the Muslim Mosque, Inc. and the Organization of Afro-American Unity. Less than a year later, he was assassinated in Washington Heights on the first day of National Brotherhood Week.
Luther, Martin	Luther, Martin was a German monk, theologian, and church reformer. He is also considered to be the founder of Protestantism. . According to him, salvation was attainable only by faith in Jesus as the Messiah, a faith unmediated by the church. These ideas helped to inspire the Protestant Reformation and changed the course of Western civilization. He is also known for his writings about the Jews, the nature and consequences of which are the subject of scholarly debate.
Society	A society is a grouping of individuals, which is characterized by common interest and may have distinctive culture and institutions.
Anti-Semitism	Anti-semitism is hostility toward or prejudice against Jews as a religious, racial, or ethnic group, which can range in expression from individual hatred to institutionalized, violent persecution.
Louis Farrakhan	Louis Farrakhan is the Supreme Minister of the Nation of Islam as the National Representative of Elijah Muhammad. He is also well-known as an advocate for African American interests and a critic of American society. Farrakhan currently resides in Kenwood, an affluent neighborhood on the south side of Chicago, and part time at a Nation of Islam farm in New Buffalo, Michigan.
Million Man March	The Million Man March was a Black march convened by Nation of Islam leader Louis Farrakhan in Washington, DC on October 16, 1995. The event included efforts to register African Americans to vote in US Elections and increase black involvement in volunteerism and community activism.
Organization	In sociology organization is understood as planned, coordinated and purposeful action of human beings to construct or compile a common tangible or intangible product or service.

Organization of Afro-American Unity	On June 28, 1964, six weeks after Malcolm X's return to New York from Africa, he announced the formation of the Organization of Afro-American Unity.
Immigration	Although human migration has existed for hundreds of thousands of years, immigration in the modern sense refers to movement of people from one nation-state to another, where they are not citizens.
Louise Cainkar	Louise Cainkar is Professor of Sociology at Marquette University. Her areas of research includes international migration, U.S. immigration, and immigrant integration, Arab American studies, and Muslims in the United States. She is a consulting scholar on the Social Science Research Council project, Reframing the Challenge of Migration and Security.
Gender	Gender refers to the differences between men and women. Gender identity is an individual's self-conception as being male or female, as distinguished from actual biological sex. In general, gender often refers to purely social rather than biological differences.
Politics	Politics is the process by which groups of people make decisions. Although the term is generally applied to behavior within governments, politics is observed in all human group interactions, including corporate, academic, and religious institutions.
George W. Bush	George W. Bush is the forty-third and current President of the United States of America. Originally inaugurated on January 20, 2001, Bush was elected president in the 2000 presidential election and re-elected in the 2004 presidential election. He previously served as the forty-sixth Governor of Texas from 1995 to 2000.
City	A city is an urban area with a large population and a particular administrative, legal, or historical status.
Nixon, Richard	Nixon, Richard was the thirty-seventh President of the United States, and was the only U.S. President to resign the office. Under his presidency, the United States followed a foreign policy marked by détente with the Soviet Union and by the opening of diplomatic relations with the People's Republic of China. His centrist domestic policies combined conservative rhetoric and liberal action in civil rights, environmental and economic initiatives.
Oklahoma City bombing	The Oklahoma City bombing was an attack on April 19, 1995 aimed at the Alfred P. Murrah Federal Building, a U.S. government office complex in downtown Oklahoma City, Oklahoma. The attack claimed 168 lives and left over 800 injured. Until the September 11, 2001 attacks, it was the deadliest act of terrorism on U.S. soil.
Terrorism	Terrorism is a term used to describe violence or other harmful acts committed (or threatened) against civilians by groups or persons for political, nationalist, or religious goals. As a type of unconventional warfare, terrorism means to weaken or supplant existing political landscapes through capitulation, acquiescence, or radicalization, as opposed to subversion or direct military action.
Attitude	Attitude is a hypothetical construct that represents an individual's like or dislike for an item. Attitudes are positive, negative or neutral views of an "attitude object": i.e. a person, behavior or event. People can also be "ambivalent" towards a target, meaning that they simultaneously possess a positive and a negative bias towards the attitude in question.
Bureau of Citizenship and Immigration Services	The Bureau of Citizenship and Immigration Services is actually a dated name for a bureau in the United States Department of Homeland Security. It performs many of the functions formerly carried out by the United States Immigration and Naturalization Service, which was part of the Department of Justice. Its priorities are to promote national security, to eliminate immigration case backlogs, and improve customer services.
Citizenship	Citizenship is membership in a society, community, or and carries with it rights to political participation; a person having such membership is a citizen.

Go to **Cram101.com** for the Practice Tests for this Chapter.

Department of Justice	The United States Department of Justice is a Cabinet department in the United States government designed to enforce the law and defend the interests of the United States according to the law and to ensure fair and impartial administration of justice for all Americans.
Justice	Justice concerns the proper ordering of things and persons within a society. As a concept it has been subject to philosophical, legal, and theological reflection and debate throughout history.
PATRIOT Act	The Patriot Act is a controversial Act of Congress which U.S. President George W. Bush signed into law on October 26, 2001. Passed with minimal debate only 45 days after the September 11, 2001 attacks on the World Trade Center in New York City, the Act dramatically expanded the authority of U.S. law enforcement agencies for the stated purpose of fighting terrorism in the United States and abroad.
American Arab Anti Discrimination Committee	The American Arab Anti Discrimination Committee is a grassroots civil rights organization open to all regardless of background, faith and ethnicity committed to defending the rights of people of Arab descent and promoting their rich cultural heritage.
Committee	A committee is a type of small deliberative assembly that is usually subordinate to another, larger deliberative assembly.
Prejudice	Prejudice is, as the name implies, the process of "pre-judging" something. It implies coming to a judgment on a subject before learning where the preponderance of evidence actually lies, or forming a judgment without direct experience.
Ritter	Ritter is the second-lowest-ranking title of nobility in German-speaking areas, just above an Edler, considered roughly equal to the title Knight or Baronet.
Discrimination	Discrimination refers to the denial of equal access to social resources to people on the basis of their group membership.

Model minority	Model minority refers to a minority ethnic, racial, or religious group whose members achieve a higher degree of success than the population average. This success is typically measured in income, education, and related factors such as low crime rate and high family stability.
Minority	A minority is a sociological group that does not constitute a politically dominant plurality of the total population of a given society. A sociological minority is not necessarily a numerical minority it may include any group that is disadvantaged with respect to a dominant group in terms of social status, education, employment, wealth and political power.
Stereotype	A stereotype is a simplified and/or standardized conception or image with specific meaning, often held in common by one group of people about another group. A stereotype can be a conventional and oversimplified conception, opinion, or image, based on the assumption that there are attributes that members of the other group hold in common. Stereotypes may be positive or negative in tone. They are typically generalizations based on minimal or limited
Strauss	Strauss was an American sociologist, who worked the field of medical sociology. Strauss is best known for his work on the methodology in qualitative research and in particular for the development of grounded theory, a general methodology he established together with Barney Glaser in the 1960s.
Edna Bonacich	Edna Bonacich is Professor of Sociology and Ethnic Studies at the University of California, Riverside. Her major research interest has been the study of class and race, with emphasis on racial divisions in the working class. One of her books is The Garment Industry in the Restructuring Global Economy.
John Modell	John Modell is Professor of Education and Sociology at the Brown Research. His research interest are sociology of childhood, adolescence and youth, sociology of education, and history of social and behavioral science. He seeks to understand the way lifetimes are put together. It is organized both socially and morally required to be formally educated during much of one's first two decades of life.
Consortium	A consortium is an association of two or more individuals, companies, organizations or governments or any combination of these entities with the objective of participating in a common activity or pooling their resources for achieving a common goal.
Ethnic identity	Ethnic identity refers to an enduring, basic aspect of the self that includes a sense of membership in an ethnic group and the attitudes and feelings related to that membership. Ethnic identity can vary with changes in social context.
Mass media	Mass media refers to forms of communication designed to reach a vast audience without any personal contact between the senders and receivers.
Yellow peril	Yellow Peril was a color metaphor for race that originated in the late nineteenth century with immigration of Chinese laborers to various Western countries, notably the United States, and later to the Japanese during the mid 20th century due to Japanese military expansion.
Identity	Identity is an umbrella term used throughout the social sciences to describe an individual's comprehension of him or herself as a discrete, separate entity.
Media	In communication, media are the storage and transmission tools used to store and deliver information or data. It is often referred to as synonymous with mass media or news media, but may refer to a single medium used to communicate any data for any purpose.
Violence	Violence is, on the one hand, acts of aggression and abuse that cause' or intend to cause injury to person or persons. Central to this concept of violence is the presence of the definite intention to cause significant injury, damage and harm.
Racial profiling	Racial profiling is inclusion of race in the profile of a persons considered likely to commit a particular crime or type of crime.

Cultural diversity	Cultural diversity is the variety of human societies or cultures in a specific region, or in the world as a whole.
Spanish American War	The Spanish American War was an armed military conflict between Spain and the United States that took place from April to August 1898. The war began due to American demands that Spain peacefully resolve the Cuban fight for independence, though strong expansionist sentiment in the United States may have also motivated the government to target Spain's other remaining overseas territories: Puerto Rico, the Philippines, Guam and the Caroline Islands.
Immigration	Although human migration has existed for hundreds of thousands of years, immigration in the modern sense refers to movement of people from one nation-state to another, where they are not citizens.
Yen Le Espiritu	Yen Le Espiritu is Professor and Chair of the Department of Ethnic Studies. She specializes in U.S. imperialism and wars, Southeast Asian refugees, and Filipino American history. She is interested on the transnational and gendered lives of Filipino immigrants and Filipino Americans.
Cultural identity	Cultural identity is the identity of a group or culture, or of an individual as far as he/she is influenced by his/her belonging to a group or culture. It is similar to and has overlaps with, but is not synonymous with, identity politics.
David Riesman	David Riesman, was a United States sociologist, attorney, and educator.
Vietnamese American	A Vietnamese American is a resident of the United States who is of Vietnamese heritage. They make up about half of all overseas Vietnamese and are the fourth-largest Asian American group.
Refugee	According to the 1951 United Nations Convention Relating to the Status of a Refugee, a refugee is a person who owing to a well-founded fear of being persecuted for reasons of race, religion, nationality, membership of a particular social group, or political opinion, is outside the country of their nationality, and is unable to or, owing to such fear, is unwilling to avail him/herself of the protection of that country.
Crime	A normative definition views crime as deviant behavior that violates prevailing norms, specifically, cultural standards prescribing how humans ought to behave.
Hmong	Hmong refers to an Asian ethnic group in the mountainous regions of southern China. Beginning in the 18th-century, Hmong groups began a gradual mass migration to Southeast Asia for reasons both political and economic.
Wisconsin	Wisconsin is a state located near the center of the North American continent. It touches two of the five Great Lakes and is one of the fifty states that constitute the United States of America. Wisconsin's capital is Madison, and its largest city is Milwaukee. Jim Doyle has been the Governor of Wisconsin since January 6, 2003.
Case study	Case study refers to a research design that focuses on a single example rather than a representative sample.
Community	A community is a social group of organisms sharing an environment, normally with shared interests. In human communities, intent, belief, resources, preferences, needs, risks and a number of other conditions may be present and common, affecting the identity of the participants and their degree of cohesiveness.
Korean	The Korean people are an East Asian ethnic group. Archaeological evidence suggest proto-Korean were Altaic language speaking migrants from south-central Siberia, who populated ancient Korea in successive waves from neolithic age to Bronze Age. The language of the Korean people is the Korean language, which uses hangul as its main writing system. There are around 73 million speakers of the Korean language worldwide.

Ethnic group	An ethnic group is a population of human beings whose members identify with each other, usually on the basis of a presumed common genealogy or ancestry. Ethnicity is also defined from the recognition by others as a distinct group and by common cultural, linguistic, religious, behavioral or biological traits.
Groups	In sociology, a group can be defined as two or more humans that interact with one another, accept expectations and obligations as members of the group, and share a common identity. By this definition, society can be viewed as a large group, though most social groups are considerably smaller.
Sovereignty	Sovereignty is the exclusive right to exercise supreme political (e.g. legislative, judicial, and/or executive) authority over a geographic region, group of people, or oneself.
Panethnicity	Panethnicity is the grouping together and labeling of various ethnicities into one all-encompassing group.

Chinese Americans	Chinese Americans are Americans of Chinese descent. Chinese Americans constitute one group of Overseas Chinese and are a subgroup of Asian Americans.
Japanese Americans	Japanese Americans are Americans of Japanese descent who trace their ancestry to Japan or Okinawa and are residents and/or citizens of the United States.
Population	A population is the collection of people or organisms of a particular species living in a given geographic area or space, usually measured by a census.
Chinese Exclusion Act	The Chinese Exclusion Act was a United States federal law passed on May 6, 1882, following 1880 revisions to the Burlingame Treaty of 1868. Those revisions allowed the U.S. to suspend immigration, and Congress subsequently acted quickly to implement the suspension of Chinese
Community	A community is a social group of organisms sharing an environment, normally with shared interests. In human communities, intent, belief, resources, preferences, needs, risks and a number of other conditions may be present and common, affecting the identity of the participants and their degree of cohesiveness.
Clan	A clan is a group of people united by kinship and descent, which is defined by perceived descent from a common ancestor found in many pre-industrial societies.
Stanford M. Lyman	Stanford M. Lyman was a scholars' scholar, prolific author, and recognized authority on ethnic minorites and race relations. He also held the Robert R. Morrow Eminent Scholar Chair in Social Science at Florida Atlantic University. He is credited with inaugurating Asian-American Studies in the United States as a result of a course he taught at the University of California, Berkeley.
Tongs	Tongs are similar to triads except that they originated among the early immigrant Chinatown communities rather than an extention of a modern triad in China. The first tongs formed in the second half of the 19th century among the more marginalized members of early immigrant Chinese American communities for mutual support and protection from white racists.
Sweatshop	Sweatshop is a pejorative term used to describe a manufacturing facility, usually a garment manufacturing facility, where working conditions are poor and workers are paid little. It has proved a difficult issue to resolve because their roots lie in the conceptual foundations of the world economy.
Social problem	A social condition that is perceived as having harmful effects is a social problem. Opinions about whether a condition is a social problem vary among groups and depend upon how and by whom the condition is defined and perceived in society.
Gang	A gang is a group of individuals who share a common identity and, in current usage, engage in illegal activities. Historically the term referred to both criminal groups and ordinary groups of friends.
Issei	Issei is a term used in countries in North and South America to specify Japanese people who emigrated to other countries in the years preceding World War II. The term issei Japanese American refers specifically to issei living in the United States.
Kibei	Kibei was a term often used in the 1940s to describe Japanese Americans born in the United States who returned to America after receiving their education in Japan.
Nisei	Nisei are people, or a person, of Japanese ancestry and the first generation to be born abroad.
Sansei	Sansei is a term used in North and South America to specify the child of a Nisei couple.
Ronald Takaki	Ronald Takaki is an ethnic studies historian. His work helps dispel stereotypes of Asian Americans such as the model minority myth. He was inspired to fight for equality for the Asian American community from his personal experiences. Early in his life he faced

discrimination as a college student in midwestern America.

Yonsei	Yonsei is a term used in geographic areas outside of Japan to specify the child of at least one Sansei parent.
Edna Bonacich	Edna Bonacich is Professor of Sociology and Ethnic Studies at the University of California, Riverside. Her major research interest has been the study of class and race, with emphasis on racial divisions in the working class. One of her books is The Garment Industry in the Restructuring Global Economy.
Citizenship	Citizenship is membership in a society, community, or and carries with it rights to political participation; a person having such membership is a citizen.
Executive Order	An executive order in the United States is a directive issued by the President, the head of the executive branch of the federal government. In other countries, similar edicts may be known as decrees, or orders-in-council.
Executive Order 9066	The Executive Order 9066 was a presidential executive order issued during World War II by U.S. President Franklin D. Roosevelt, using his authority as Commander-in-Chief to exercise war powers to send ethnic groups to internment camps. The order led to the Japanese American internment in which some 120,000 ethnic Japanese people were held in internment camps for the duration of the war.
Japanese American Citizens League	The Japanese American Citizens League was formed in 1929 to protect the rights of Japanese Americans from the state and federal governments. It fought for civil rights for Japanese Americans, assisted those in internment camps during World War II, and led a successful campaign for redress for internment from the U.S. Congress.
Evacuation	Emergency evacuation is the movement of persons from a dangerous place due to the threat or occurrence of a disastrous event. Examples inc lude the evacuation of a building due to a bomb threat or fire, the evacuation of a district because of a flood or bombardment, or an evacuation from a city due to a hurricane. In situations involving hazardous materials or possible contamination, evacuees may be decontaminated prior to being transported out of the contaminated area.
Gene	A gene is a locatable region of genomic sequence, corresponding to a unit of inheritance, which is associated with regulatory regions, transcribed regions and/or other functional sequence regions. A gene is a union of genomic sequences encoding a coherent set of potentially overlapping functional products.
Loyalty	Loyalty is faithfulness or a devotion to a person or cause.
Security	Security is the condition of being protected against danger or loss.
Internment	Internment is the imprisonment or confinement of people, commonly in large groups, without trial. It also refers to the practice of neutral countries in time of war in detaining belligerent armed forces and equipment in their territories under the Second Hague Convention.
George W. Bush	George W. Bush is the forty-third and current President of the United States of America. Originally inaugurated on January 20, 2001, Bush was elected president in the 2000 presidential election and re-elected in the 2004 presidential election. He previously served as the forty-sixth Governor of Texas from 1995 to 2000.
Civil Liberties	Civil liberties are freedoms that protect the individual from government to a certain extent.
Reagan, Ronald	Reagan, Ronald implemented new political initiatives as well as economic policies, advocating a laissez-faire philosophy, but the extent to which these ideas were implemented is debatable. He ordered a massive military buildup in an arms race with the Soviet Union, rejecting the previous strategy of détente and directly confronting Communism.

Thomas M. Shapiro	Thomas M. Shapiro is a professor of Sociology and Public Policy at Brandeis University and is the author The Hidden Costs of Being African American. His primary areas of focus and publications are racial inequality and public policy.
Religion	A religion is a set of common beliefs and practices generally held by a group of people, often codified as prayer, ritual, and religious law. Religion also encompasses ancestral or cultural traditions, writings, history, and mythology, as well as personal faith and mystic experience.
Stereotype	A stereotype is a simplified and/or standardized conception or image with specific meaning, often held in common by one group of people about another group. A stereotype can be a conventional and oversimplified conception, opinion, or image, based on the assumption that there are attributes that members of the other group hold in common. Stereotypes may be positive or negative in tone. They are typically generalizations based on minimal or limited knowledge about a group to which the person doing the stereotyping does not belong. Persons may be grouped based on race, ethnicity, religion, sexual orientation, or any number of other
Discrimination	Discrimination refers to the denial of equal access to social resources to people on the basis of their group membership.
Prejudice	Prejudice is, as the name implies, the process of "pre-judging" something. It implies coming to a judgment on a subject before learning where the preponderance of evidence actually lies, or forming a judgment without direct experience.
Civil Rights	Civil rights are the protections and privileges of personal liberty given to all citizens by law. Civil rights are rights that are bestowed by nations on those within their territorial boundaries.
Mass media	Mass media refers to forms of communication designed to reach a vast audience without any personal contact between the senders and receivers.
Cultural diversity	Cultural diversity is the variety of human societies or cultures in a specific region, or in the world as a whole.
Media	In communication, media are the storage and transmission tools used to store and deliver information or data. It is often referred to as synonymous with mass media or news media, but may refer to a single medium used to communicate any data for any purpose.

Orthodoxy	Orthodoxy is typically used to refer to the correct worship or the correct theological and doctrinal observance of religion, or other forms of intellectual activity shared by organizations or movements, as determined by some overseeing body
Lawsuit	In American law, a lawsuit is a civil or criminal action brought before a court in which the party commencing the action, the plaintiff, seeks a legal remedy. One or more defendants are required to respond to the plaintiff's complaint. If the plaintiff is successful, judgment will be given in the plaintiff's favor, and a range of court orders may be issued to enforce a right, award damages, or impose an injunction to prevent an act or compel an act.
Population	A population is the collection of people or organisms of a particular species living in a given geographic area or space, usually measured by a census.
Jewish Americans	Jewish Americans are Jews who are American citizens or resident aliens. The United States is home to the largest or second largest Jewish community in the world depending on religious definitions and varying population data.
Ethnic identity	Ethnic identity refers to an enduring, basic aspect of the self that includes a sense of membership in an ethnic group and the attitudes and feelings related to that membership. Ethnic identity can vary with changes in social context.
Identity	Identity is an umbrella term used throughout the social sciences to describe an individual's comprehension of him or herself as a discrete, separate entity.
Ashley Montagu	Ashley Montagu, was a British-American anthropologist and humanist who popularized issues such as race and gender and their relation to politics and development. He was the rapporteur, in 1950, of the UNESCO statement The Race Question.
Immigration	Although human migration has existed for hundreds of thousands of years, immigration in the modern sense refers to movement of people from one nation-state to another, where they are not citizens.
Citizenship	Citizenship is membership in a society, community, or and carries with it rights to political participation; a person having such membership is a citizen.
Marshal	Marshal is a word used in several official titles of various branches of society. As they became trusted members of the courts of Medieval Europe, the title grew in reputation. During the last few centuries, it has been used for the most elevated offices.
Genocide	Genocide is the deliberate and systematic destruction of an ethnic, religious or national group. It is define as "any of the following acts committed with intent to destroy, in whole or in part, a national, ethnical, racial or religious group, as such: killing members of the group; causing serious bodily or mental harm to members of the group; deliberately inflicting on the group conditions of life, calculated to bring about its physical destruction in whole or in part; imposing measures intended to prevent births within the group; forcibly transferring children of the group to another group."
Migration	The movement of people from one country or region to another in order to settle permanently, is referred to as a migration.
Gordon W. Allport	Gordon W. Allport was an American psychologist. He rejected both a psychoanalytic approach to personality, which he thought often went too deep, and a behavioral approach, which he thought often did not go deep enough. He was one of the first researchers to draw a distinction between Motive and Drive. He suggested that a drive formed as a reaction to a motive may out-grow the motive as a reason.
Anti-Semitism	Anti-semitism is hostility toward or prejudice against Jews as a religious, racial, or ethnic group, which can range in expression from individual hatred to institutionalized, violent persecution.

Holocaust	The Holocaust is the term generally used to describe the killing of approximately six million European Jews during World War II, as part of a program of deliberate extermination planned and executed by the National Socialist regime in Germany led by Adolf Hitler.
In-group	In sociology, an in-group is a social group towards which an individual feels loyalty and respect, usually due to membership in the group.
Merton	Merton coined the phrase "self-fulfilling prophecy." He also coined many other phrases that have gone into everyday use, such as "role model" and "unintended consequences".
Vice	Vice is a practice or habit that is considered immoral, depraved, and/or degrading in the associated society.
Life is Beautiful	Life Is Beautiful is a 1997 Italian language film which tells the story of a Jewish Italian, Guido Orefice, who must learn how to use his fertile imagination to help his son survive their internment in a Nazi concentration camp.
Anti-Defamation League	The Anti-Defamation League is an advocacy group founded in 1913 by B'nai B'rith in the United States whose stated aim is "to stop, by appeals to reason and conscience and, if necessary, by appeals to law, the defamation of the Jewish people. Its ultimate purpose is to secure justice and fair treatment to all citizens alike and to put an end forever to unjust and unfair discrimination against and ridicule of any sect or body of citizens."
Henry Ford	Henry Ford was the American founder of the Ford Motor Company and father of modern assembly lines used in mass production. His introduction of the Model T automobile revolutionized transportation and American industry. He was a prolific inventor and was awarded 161 U.S. patents. As owner of the Ford Company he became one of the richest and best-known people in the world. He is credited with "Fordism", that is, the mass production of large numbers of inexpensive automobiles using the assembly line, coupled with high wages for his workers. Ford had a global vision, with consumerism as the key to peace. Ford did not believe in accountants; he amassed one of the world's largest fortunes without ever having his company audited under his administration. Henry Ford's intense commitment to lowering costs
German American Bund	The German American Bund was an American Nazi organization established in the 1930s. Its main goal was to promote a favorable view of the Nazi Germany. It was one of several German-American heritage groups; however, it was one of the few to express National Socialist ideals. As a result, many considered the group anti-American.
Independent	The independent variables are those that are deliberately manipulated to invoke a change in the dependent variables. In short, "if x is given, then y occurs", where x represents the independent variables and y represents the dependent variables.
Charles Lindbergh	Charles Lindbergh was an American aviator, author, inventor, explorer, and peace activist who rose instantaneously from virtual obscurity to world fame as the result of his piloting of the first solo nonstop Transatlantic flight from New York. He also became a leader of the anti-war America First movement. Nonetheless, he supported the war effort after Pearl Harbor and flew many combat missions in the Pacific Theater as a civilian consultant.
Liberation	Liberation is based on the word liberty, related to the word liberal, and it is often understood as "to be freed from not having freedom to having freedom".
Organization	In sociology organization is understood as planned, coordinated and purposeful action of human beings to construct or compile a common tangible or intangible product or service.
African Americans	African Americans are citizens or residents of the United States whose ancestors, usually in predominant part, were indigenous to Sub-Saharan Africa. Most are the descendants of captive Africans who were enslaved within the boundaries of the present United States.
Diaspora	The dispersal of an ethnic population from an original homeland into foreign areas, often in

Go to **Cram101.com** for the Practice Tests for this Chapter.

	a forced manner or under traumatic circumstances, is referred to as a diaspora.
Zionism	Zionism is an international political movement that supports a homeland for the Jewish people in the Land of Israel. Formally organized in the late 19th century, the movement was successful in establishing the State of Israel in 1948, as the world's first and only modern Jewish State.
James Arthur Baldwin	James Arthur Baldwin was an American novelist, writer, playwright, poet, essayist, and civil rights activist.
Black Panther party	The Black Panther Party was an African-American organization established to promote civil rights and self-defense. It was active in the United States from the mid-1960s into the 1970s.
Louis Farrakhan	Louis Farrakhan is the Supreme Minister of the Nation of Islam as the National Representative of Elijah Muhammad. He is also well-known as an advocate for African American interests and a critic of American society. Farrakhan currently resides in Kenwood, an affluent neighborhood on the south side of Chicago, and part time at a Nation of Islam farm in New Buffalo, Michigan.
Jesse Jackson	Jesse Jackson is an American civil rights activist and Baptist minister. He was a candidate for the Democratic presidential nomination in 1984 and 1988 and served as "shadow senator" for the District of Columbia from 1991 to 1997. He was the founder of both entities that merged to form Rainbow/PUSH. Representative Jesse Jackson, Jr. is his eldest son.
Income	Income, generally defined, is the money that is received as a result of the normal business activities of an individual or a business.
American Indians	American Indians are the indigenous peoples from the regions of North America now encompassed by the continental United States, including parts of Alaska. They comprise a large number of distinct tribes, states, and ethnic groups, many of which survive as intact political communities. There has been a wide range of terms used to describe them and no consensus has been reached among indigenous members as to what they prefer.
American Jewish Congress	The American Jewish Congress describes itself as an association of Jewish Americans organized to defend Jewish interests at home and abroad through public policy advocacy, using diplomacy, legislation, and the courts
Appeal	In law, an appeal is a process for making a formal challenge to an official decision. Depending on circumstances, it may be made to the same authority or to a higher judicial authority.
Committee	A committee is a type of small deliberative assembly that is usually subordinate to another, larger deliberative assembly.
Congress	In politics, a congress "a gathering of people" is the name of the main legislative body in a state that operates under a congressional system of government. In non-political usage congress is a term applied to a large national or international grouping of people meeting together with common interests or concerns, e.g. an academic conference.
Abraham Lavender	Abraham Lavender is a professor of Sociology at Florida International University, and is president of the Society for Crypto-Judaic Studies. He earned his PhD writing his dissertation on The Generational Hypothesis of Jewish Identity: The Return of the Third Generation.
Native Americans	Native Americans in the United States are the indigenous peoples from the regions of North America now encompassed by the continental United States, including parts of Alaska. They comprise a large number of distinct tribes, states, and ethnic groups, many of which are still enduring as political communities.

Language	A language is a system of symbols and the rules used to manipulate them. Language can also refer to the use of such systems as a general phenomenon. Because a language also has a grammar, it can manipulate its symbols to express clear and regular relationships between them.
George W. Bush	George W. Bush is the forty-third and current President of the United States of America. Originally inaugurated on January 20, 2001, Bush was elected president in the 2000 presidential election and re-elected in the 2004 presidential election. He previously served as the forty-sixth Governor of Texas from 1995 to 2000.
Steven M. Cohen	Steven M. Cohen is a sociologist of American Jewry. He is Professor of Jewish Social Policy at Hebrew Union College - Jewish Institute of Religion, New York. He is well known for his book The Jew Within: Self, Family, and Community in the United States. He has authored and done articles exploring patterns of Jewish identity and community in the U.S. and elsewhere.
Al Gore	Al Gore is an American environmental activist, author, businessperson, and former politician.
Judaism	Judaism is the religion of the Jewish people, based on principles and ethics embodied in the Bible and the Talmud. It is among the oldest religious traditions still in practice today. While Judaism has seldom, if ever, been monolithic in practice, it has always been monotheistic in theology. It differs from many religions in that central authority is not vested in a person or group, but in sacred texts and traditions.
Politics	Politics is the process by which groups of people make decisions. Although the term is generally applied to behavior within governments, politics is observed in all human group interactions, including corporate, academic, and religious institutions.
Reform	A reform movement is a kind of social movement that aims to make gradual change, or change in certain aspects of society rather than rapid or fundamental changes.
Shadchan	Shadchan is a Yiddish word for matchmaker.
Marginalization	Marginalization refers to the overt or covert trends within societies whereby those perceived as lacking desirable traits or deviating from the group norms tend to be excluded by wider society and ostracised as undesirables.
Calvin Goldscheider	Calvin Goldscheider is Professor of Sociology and Ungerleider Professor of Judaic Studies at Brown University. He is the author of Cultures in Conflict: The Arab-Israeli Conflict. His major research publications have focused on the sociology and demography of ethnic populations, historically and comparatively with emphasis on family and immigration.
Sidney Goldstein	Sidney Goldstein is the founder and director of the Population Studies and Training Center. He is an internationally recognized expert on internal migration and urbanization. His research focuses on population distribution, urbanization, types of migrations, and the interrelations between migration and fertility. Much of his wokr had focused on Southeast Asia and China and had done research on the demography of Jews.
Denomination	The third most powerful type of religious institution, with a membership generally dominated by a single social class, a formal but not bureaucratic role structure, a trained clergy, traditional authority, abstract relatively unemotional ritual, and a condition of coexistence between it and dominant political and economic institutions, is referred to as a denomination.
Milton Gordon	Milton Gordon is an American sociologist. He is most noted for having devised a theory on the Seven Stages of Assimilation.

Go to **Cram101.com** for the Practice Tests for this Chapter.

American Dilemma	An American Dilemma: The Negro Problem and Modern Democracy is a 1944 study of race relations authored by Swedish economist Gunnar Myrdal and funded by The Carnegie Foundation. The foundation chose Myrdal because it thought that as a non-American, he could offer a more
Hacker	In a security context, a hacker is someone involved in computer security/insecurity, specializing in the discovery of exploits in systems (for exploitation or prevention), or in obtaining or preventing unauthorized access to systems through skills, tactics and detailed knowledge.
Myrdal, Gunnar	Myrdal, Gunnar was a Swedish economist and politician. He, along with Friedrich von Hayek, won the Nobel Prize for Economics for their "pioneering work in the theory of money and economic fluctuations and for their penetrating analysis of the interdependence of economic, social and institutional phenomena." He was also known for his study, An American Dilemma: The Negro Problem and Modern Democracy, which influenced the US Supreme Court decision in
Status	In sociology or anthropology, social status is the honor or prestige attached to one's position in society one's social position. The stratification system, which is the system of distributing rewards to the members of society, determines social status. Social status, the position or rank of a person or group within the stratification system, can be determined two ways. One can earn their social status by their own achievements, which is known as achieved status, or one can be placed in the stratification system by their inherited position, which is called ascribed status.
Minority	A minority is a sociological group that does not constitute a politically dominant plurality of the total population of a given society. A sociological minority is not necessarily a numerical minority it may include any group that is disadvantaged with respect to a dominant group in terms of social status, education, employment, wealth and political power.
Patti Adler	Patti Adler is considered to be one of the top experts in the field of Sociological Deviance and one of the best-known professors at the University of Colorado at Boulder. She currently teaches a class, Deviance in US Society, which enrolls 500 people every semester. She also teaches undergraduate and graduate courses in field research methods, and is a leading internationally known writer and speaker on this topic.
Androgyny	Androgyny refers to the blending of traditional feminine and masculine traits.
Gender	Gender refers to the differences between men and women. Gender identity is an individual's self-conception as being male or female, as distinguished from actual biological sex. In general, gender often refers to purely social rather than biological differences.
Gender role	A gender role is a set of perceived behavioral norms associated particularly with males or females, in a given social group or system.
Sexism	Sexism is commonly considered to be discrimination and/or hatred against people based on their sex rather than their individual merits, but can also refer to any and all systemic differentiations based on the sex of the individuals.
Social role	A social role is a set of connected behaviors, rights and obligations as conceptualized by actors in a social situation. It is mostly defined as an expected behavior in a given individual social status and social position.
Disability	Disability is lack of ability relative to a personal or group standard or spectrum. Disability may involve physical impairment, sensory impairment, cognitive or intellectual impairment, mental disorder also known as psychiatric disability, or various types of chronic disease. A disability may occur during a person's lifetime or may be present from birth.
Parsons	Parsons was an advocate of "grand theory," an attempt to integrate all the social sciences into an overarching theoretical framework. His early work — The Structure of Social Action —reviewed the output of his great predecessors, especially Max Weber, Vilfredo Pareto, and

Go to Cram101.com for the Practice Tests for this Chapter.

	Émile Durkheim, and attempted to derive from them a single "action theory" based on the assumptions that human action is voluntary, intentional, and symbolic.
Talcott Parsons	Talcott Parsons was for many years the best-known sociologist in the United States, and indeed one of the best-known in the world. His work was very influential through the 1950s and well into the 1960s, particularly in the United States, but fell gradually out of favour afterward.
Sex	Sex refers to the male and female duality of biology and reproduction. Unlike organisms that only have the ability to reproduce asexually, male and female pairs have the ability to produce offspring through meiosis and fertilization.
Sexual differentiation	Sexual differentiation is the process of development of the differences between males and females from an undifferentiated zygote.
Differentiation	Differentiation is a term in system theory, from the viewpoint of this theory the principal feature of modern society is the increased process of system differentiation as a way of dealing with the complexity of its environment. This is accomplished through the creation of subsystems in an effort to copy within a system the difference between it and the environment.
Sociological perspective	The sociological perspective is a particular way of approaching a phenomena common in sociology. It involves maintaining objectivity, not by divesting oneself of values, but by critically evaluating and testing ideas, and accepting what may be surprizing or even displeasing based on the evidence. The sociological perspective often assumes that "official" explanations are incomplete or self-serving.
Feminism	Feminism is a diverse collection of social theories, political movements and moral philosophies, largely motivated by or concerned with the experiences of women.
Feminist movement	The feminist movement is a series of campaigns on issues such as reproductive rights, domestic violence, maternity leave, equal pay, sexual harassment, and sexual violence. The goals of the movement vary from country to country, e.g. opposition to female genital cutting in Sudan, or to the glass ceiling in Western countries.
Lucretia Mott	Lucretia Mott was an American Quaker minister, abolitionist, social reformer and proponent of women's rights. She is credited as the first American "feminist" in the early 1800s but was, more accurately, the initiator of women's political advocacy. Her husband supported her activism and they often sheltered runaway slaves in their home. They co-founded the Pennsylvania Anti-Slavery Society and she also founded the Philadelphia Female Anti-Slavery Society.
Elizabeth Cady Stanton	Elizabeth Cady Stanton was an American social activist and leading figure of the early woman's movement. Her Declaration of Sentiments, presented at the first women's rights convention held in 1848 in Seneca Falls, New York, is often credited with initiating the first organized woman's rights and woman's suffrage movements in the United States.
Suffrage	Suffrage is the civil right to vote, or the exercise of that right. In that context, it is also called political franchise or simply the franchise, a term dating from the time when the Franks of ancient France were free.
Birth control	Birth control is a regimen of one or more actions, devices, or medications followed in order to deliberately prevent or reduce the likelihood of a woman giving birth or becoming pregnant.
Jo Freeman	Jo Freeman is an American feminist and scholar noted for her feminist activism in the 1960s and 1970s. is the author of The Tyranny of Structurelessness, a pamphlet critical of the "structureless" organizing models employed by the women's movement during that time.

Go to **Cram101.com** for the Practice Tests for this Chapter.

Nineteenth Amendment	The Nineteenth Amendment to the United States Constitution provides that neither the individual states of the United States nor its federal government may deny a citizen the right to vote because of the citizen's sex.
Margaret Sanger	Margaret Sanger was an American birth control activist, an advocate of negative eugenics, and the founder of the American Birth Control League. In her drive to open the way to universal access to birth control, she was ahead of her time. However, her racist ideology and advocacy for eugenics are positions which have tarnished her reputation.
Liberation	Liberation is based on the word liberty, related to the word liberal, and it is often understood as "to be freed from not having freedom to having freedom".
Feminine mystique	The Feminine Mystique is a 1963 book written by Betty Friedan which attacked the popular notion that women of that time could only find fulfillment through childbearing and homemaking. According to The New York Times obituary of Friedan in 2006, it "ignited the contemporary women's movement in 1963 and as a result permanently transformed the social fabric of the United States and countries around the world" and "is widely regarded as one of the most influential nonfiction books of the 20th century."
Myra Marx Ferree	Myra Marx Ferree is a professor of sociology and director of the Center for German and European Studies at the University of Wisconsin-Madison. She has written numerous articles about feminist organizations and politics in the US, Germany and internationally, as well as about gender inequality in families, the inclusion of gender in sociological theory and practice, and the intersections of gender with race and class.
Betty Friedan	Betty Friedan was an American feminist, activist and writer, best known for starting what is commonly known as the "Second Wave" of feminism through the writing of her book The Feminine Mystique.
Arlie Russell Hochschild	Arlie Russell Hochschild is a professor of sociology at the University of California, Berkeley. She is the author of several prize-winning books and numerous articles which discuss the dual labor by women in both the general economy and within the household. In her essay, "Love and Gold" in Global Woman: Nannies, Maids and Sex Workers in the New Economy, she sets the concept of emotional labor in a larger political context.
Marx	Marx was a 19th century philosopher, political economist, and revolutionary. Marx addressed a wide range of political as well as social issues ; he is most famous for his analysis of history, summed up in the opening line of the Communist Manifesto: "The history of all hitherto existing society is the history of class struggles". Marx believed that capitalism would be displaced by radical socialism which in turn would develop into a communism.
National Organization for Women	The National Organization for Women is the largest American feminist organization. It was founded in 1966 and has a membership of 500,000 contributing members and 550 chapters in all 50 U.S. states and the District of Columbia.
Organization	In sociology organization is understood as planned, coordinated and purposeful action of human beings to construct or compile a common tangible or intangible product or service.
Labor	In economics, labor is a measure of the work done by human beings. It is conventionally contrasted with such other factors of production as land and capital. There are theories which have created a concept called human capital, although there are also counter posing macro-economic system theories that think human capital is a contradiction in terms.
Labor force	In economics the people in the labor force are the suppliers of labor. The fraction of the labor force that is seeking work but cannot find it determines the unemployment rate. The labor force participation rate is the ratio between the labor force and the overall size of their cohort.
Segregation	Segregation may be mandated by law or exist through social norms. Segregation may be

	maintained by means ranging from discrimination in hiring and in the rental and sale of housing to certain races to vigilante violence such as lynchings; a situation that arises when members of different races mutually prefer to associate and do business with members of their own race would usually be described as separation or de facto separation of the races rather than segregation.
Day care	Day care is a term used to describe the care of a child during the day by a person other than the child's parents or legal guardians, typically someone outside the child's immediate family.
Civil Rights	Civil rights are the protections and privileges of personal liberty given to all citizens by law. Civil rights are rights that are bestowed by nations on those within their territorial boundaries.
Equal Employment Opportunity Commission	The Equal Employment Opportunity Commission is a United States federal agency tasked with ending employment discrimination in the United States. It also serves as an adjudicatory for claims of discrimination brought against federal agencies.
Pay equity	Pay equity is a method of eliminating discrimination against women who are paid less than men for jobs requiring comparable levels of expertise. A policy to establish pay equity usuallys refers to that all jobs will be evaluated and given points according to the level of knowledge and responsibility required to do the job and that salary adjustments will be made if its discovered that women are consistently paid less then men for jobs with similar points.
Equity	Equity is the concept or idea of fairness in economics, particularly as to taxation or welfare economics.
Mommy track	Mommy track is a term used to describe the lifestyle of women who choose to leave the workforce in order to pursue childbearing. This is a source of considerable political and social discussion.
Strauss	Strauss was an American sociologist, who worked the field of medical sociology. Strauss is best known for his work on the methodology in qualitative research and in particular for the development of grounded theory, a general methodology he established together with Barney Glaser in the 1960s.
Saving	In common usage, saving generally means putting money aside, for example, by putting money in the bank or investing in a pension plan. In terms of personal finance, saving refers to preserving money for future use - typically by putting it on deposit - this is distinct from investment where there is an element of risk.
Sexual harassment	Sexual harassment refers to the making of persistent unwanted sexual advances by one individual towards another.
Harassment	Harassment refers to a wide spectrum of offensive behavior. When the term is used in a legal sense it refers to behaviors that are found threatening or disturbing, and beyond those that are sanctioned by society. Sexual harassment refers to persistent and unwanted sexual advances, typically in the workplace, where the consequences of refusing are potentially very disadvantaging to the victim.
Feminization	The term feminization has been used to describe a shift in gender roles and sex roles in a society.
Feminization of poverty	The feminization of poverty has been observed since 1970 as female headed households accounted for a growing proportion of those below the poverty line. A large majority of these women are divorced or never-married mothers.

Oberlin College	Oberlin College is a private, highly selective liberal arts college in Oberlin, Ohio. Its students have a reputation for being radically liberal and/or progressive. It has a thriving LGBT community, and most students are well informed about the intricacies of gender politics.
Homemaker	Homemaker is a mainly American term which may refer either to: 1) the person within a family who is primarily concerned with the management of the household, whether or not he or she works outside the home, or; 2) a person whose prime occupation is to care for their family and/or home.
Poverty	Poverty may be seen as the collective condition of poor people, or of poor groups, and in this sense entire nation-states are sometimes regarded as poor. Although the most severe poverty is in the developing world, there is evidence of poverty in every region.
Title IX	Title IX of the Education Amendments of 1972 is a United States law enacted on June 23, 1972 that states: "No person in the United States shall, on the basis of sex, be excluded from participation in, be denied the benefits of, or be subjected to discrimination under any education program or activity receiving Federal financial assistance." Although the most prominent "public face" of Title IX is its impact on high school and collegiate athletics, the original statute made no reference to athletics. The legislation covers all educational activities, and complaints under Title IX alleging discrimination in fields such as science or math education, or in other aspects of academic life such as access to health care and dormitory facilities, are not unheard of. It also applies to non-sport activities such as
Lewis A. Coser	Lewis A. Coser was an American sociologist. Coser was the first sociologist to try to bring together structural functionalism and conflict theory; his work was focused on finding the functions of social conflict.
Rose Laub Coser	Rose Laub Coser was a sociologist and founding member of Sociologists for Women in Society. She was also a Professor Emeritus at the State University of New York at Stony Brook. She was the author of Life in the Ward and was a contributor of Sociological Studies of Health and Sickness.
Household chore	A household chore is a specific piece of work required to be done as a duty or for a specific fee, related to or used in the running of a household.
Shift work	Shift work is an employment practice designed to make use of the 24 hours of the clock, rather than a standard working day. The term shift work includes both long-term night shifts and work schedules in which employees change or rotate shifts.
Division of labor	Division of labor is the specialisation of cooperative labor in specific, circumscribed tasks and roles, intended to increase efficiency of output.
Abortion	An abortion is the removal or expulsion of an embryo or fetus from the uterus, resulting in or caused by its death. This can occur spontaneously as a miscarriage or be artificially induced by chemical, surgical or other means.
Court	A court is a public forum used by a power base to adjudicate disputes and dispense civil, labor, administrative and criminal justice under its laws. In common law and civil law states, courts are the central means for dispute resolution, and it is generally understood that all persons have an ability to bring their claims before a court. Similarly, those accused of a crime have the right to present their defense before a court.
England	England is a country, which is part of the United Kingdom. Its inhabitants account for more than 83% of the total UK population, whilst its mainland territory occupies most of the southern two-thirds of the island of Great Britain. England shares land borders with Scotland to the north and Wales to the west and elsewhere is bordered by the North Sea, Irish Sea, Celtic Sea, Bristol Channel and English Channel. The capital is London, the largest urban area in Great Britain, and the largest urban zone in the European Union by most, but not all,

measures.

Roe v. Wade	Roe v. Wade is a landmark United States Supreme Court decision establishing that most laws against abortion violate a constitutional right to privacy under the liberty clause of the Fourteenth Amendment, thus overturning all state and federal laws outlawing or restricting abortion that were inconsistent with the decision.
Court of last resort	In some countries, provinces and states, the court of last resort is the highest court whose rulings cannot be challenged.
Discrimination	Discrimination refers to the denial of equal access to social resources to people on the basis of their group membership.
Guttmacher Institute	The Guttmacher Institute is a non-profit organization which works to advance reproductive health. The institute operates in the United States and globally "through an interrelated program of social science research, policy analysis and public education." It has played a leading role in the movement for women's sexual and reproductive rights since the institute's inception.
Hyde Amendment	The Hyde Amendment is a provision barring the use of federal funds to pay for abortions for low-income women, first passed by the United States Congress in 1976.
Politics	Politics is the process by which groups of people make decisions. Although the term is generally applied to behavior within governments, politics is observed in all human group interactions, including corporate, academic, and religious institutions.
Double jeopardy	Double jeopardy is a procedural defense that forbids a defendant from being tried a second time for the same crime. At common law a defendant can plead autrefois acquit or autrefois convict; meaning the defendant has been acquitted or convicted of the same offense.
League of Women Voters	The League of Women Voters is an American political organization founded by Carrie Chapman Catt during the last meeting of the National American Woman Suffrage Association approximately six months before the Nineteenth Amendment to the United States Constitution gave U.S. women the right to vote.
Jeopardy	Jeopardy is a television quiz game show based on trivia in topics such as history, literature, pop culture, and science. The show has a decades-long broadcast history in the United States since being created by Merv Griffin in the early 1960s. It first ran on NBC from March 30, 1964 until January 3, 1975; in a weekly syndicated version from September 9, 1974 to September 7, 1975; and in a revival from October 2, 1978 to March 2, 1979. Its most successful incarnation is the Alex Trebek-hosted syndicated version, which has aired continuously since September 10, 1984. It has also been adapted internationally.
African Americans	African Americans are citizens or residents of the United States whose ancestors, usually in predominant part, were indigenous to Sub-Saharan Africa. Most are the descendants of captive Africans who were enslaved within the boundaries of the present United States.
Racism	Racism, by its simplest definition, is discrimination based on race. People with racist beliefs might hate certain groups of people according to their race, or in the case of institutional racism, certain racial groups may be denied rights or benefits. Racism typically starts with the assumption that there are taxonomic differences between different groups of people. According to the United Nations conventions, there is no distinction between the term racial discrimination and ethnic discrimination.

Aztec	Aztec is a term used to refer to certain ethnic groups of central Mexico, particularly those groups who spoke the Nahuatl language and who achieved political and military dominance over large parts of Mesoamerica in the 14th, 15th and 16th centuries, a period referred to as the
Immanuel Wallerstein	Immanuel Wallerstein is a United States sociologist. He rejected the notion of a "Third World", claiming there was only one world connected by a complex network of economic exchange relationships, in which the 'dichotomy of capital and labor', and the endless 'accumulation of capital' by competing agents account for frictions. This approach is known as the World Systems Theory.
Civilization	Civilization is a kind of human society or culture; specifically, a civilization is usually understood to be a complex society characterized by the practice of agriculture and settlement in cities. Civilization can also refer to society as a whole. To nineteenth-century English anthropologist Edward Burnett Tylor, for example, civilization was "the total social heredity of mankind."
Dominant group	The opposite of minority group, that possesses more wealth, power, and prestige in a society is a dominant group.
Race	The term race refers to the concept of dividing people into populations or groups on the basis of various sets of characteristics and beliefs about common ancestry. The most widely used human racial categories are based on visible traits especially skin color, facial features and hair texture, and self-identification.
Systems theory	A theory that emphasizes the interdependence of family members and how they affect one another is a systems theory.
Anthony DePalma	Anthony DePalma was an orthopedic surgeon, humanitarian, and teacher at Thomas Jefferson University, as well as the founder of the orthopedic department at University of Medicine and Dentistry of New Jersey. He was the first Editor-in-Chief of Clinical Orthopaedics & Related Research, a major orthopaedic journal.
Liberation	Liberation is based on the word liberty, related to the word liberal, and it is often understood as "to be freed from not having freedom to having freedom".
Mestizo	Mestizo is a Spanish term that was formerly used in the Spanish Empire and continues to be used today in Latin America and the Philippines to refer to people of mixed European and Amerindian ancestry living in the region of Latin America. The word originated from the Romance language / Latin word "Mixticius", meaning "mixed". In the Portuguese and French languages, the words "Mestiço" and "Métis" were also used in the Portuguese and French Empire to identify individuals of mixed European and Amerindian ancestry.
Mexican-American War	The Mexican-American War was an armed military conflict between the United States and Mexico in the wake of the U.S. annexation of Texas. The most important consequence of the war for the United States was the Mexican Cession, in which the Mexican territories of Alta California and Santa Fé de Nuevo México were ceded to the United States under the terms of the Treaty of Guadalupe Hidalgo. In Mexico, the enormous loss of territory following the war encouraged its government to enact policies to colonize its northern territories as a hedge against further losses.
Zapatista Army of National Liberation	The Zapatista Army of National Liberation is an armed revolutionary group based in Chiapas, one of the poorest states of Mexico. Since 1994, they have been in a declared war "against the Mexican state." Their social base is mostly indigenous but they have some supporters in urban areas as well as an international web of support.
Culture	Culture generally refers to patterns of human activity and the symbolic structures that give such activity significant importance. Culture has been called "the way of life for an entire society." As such, it includes codes of manners, dress, language, religion, rituals, norms of

behavior such as law and morality, and systems of belief.

Policy	A policy is a deliberate plan of action to guide decisions and achieve rational outcomes. The term may apply to government, private sector organizations and groups, and individuals. Presidential executive orders, corporate privacy policies, and parliamentary rules of order are all examples of policy. Policy differs from rules or law. While law can compel or prohibit behaviors policy merely guides actions toward those that are most likely to achieve a desired outcome.
Chiapas	Chiapas is the southernmost state of Mexico, located towards the southeast of the country. The state suffers from the highest rate of malnutrition in Mexico, estimated to affect more than 40% of the population. Other social issues involve the increasing presence of the Central American gangs known as Maras, and illegal immigration from Central America in general, mostly directed towards the United States, but further aggravating the panorama of local poverty. This floating influx of people is frequently subject to abuse and human rights violations from Mexican authorities.
Status	In sociology or anthropology, social status is the honor or prestige attached to one's position in society one's social position. The stratification system, which is the system of distributing rewards to the members of society, determines social status. Social status, the position or rank of a person or group within the stratification system, can be determined two ways. One can earn their social status by their own achievements, which is known as achieved status, or one can be placed in the stratification system by their inherited position, which is called ascribed status.
Maquiladora	A maquiladora is a factory that imports materials and equipment on a duty-free and tariff-free basis for assembly or manufacturing and then re-exports the assembled product, usually back to the originating country.
Multiculturalism	Multiculturalism is an ideology advocating that society should consist of, or at least allow and include, distinct cultural and religious groups, with equal status.
Cultural diversity	Cultural diversity is the variety of human societies or cultures in a specific region, or in the world as a whole.
Human	Human beings are bipedal primates in the family Hominidae. DNA evidence indicates that modern humans originated in Africa about 250,000 years ago. Humans have a highly developed brain, capable of abstract reasoning, language, introspection, and emotion. This mental capability, combined with an erect body carriage that frees the forelimbs for manipulating objects, has allowed humans to make far greater use of tools than any other species. Humans now permanently inhabit every continent on Earth, except Antarctica. Humans also now have a continuous presence in low Earth orbit, occupying the International Space Station. The human population on Earth amounts to over 6.7 billion, as of July, 2008.
Human Rights	Human rights refers to natural and inalienable rights accorded to all human beings, such as the right to life, liberty, and happiness. They also may include rights essential to a dignified human existence, such as freedom of movement, free speech, a good education, employment.
Bloc Québécois	The Bloc Québécois is a federal political party in Canada that defines itself as devoted to the promotion of sovereignty for Quebec.
Immigration	Although human migration has existed for hundreds of thousands of years, immigration in the modern sense refers to movement of people from one nation-state to another, where they are not citizens.
Minority	A minority is a sociological group that does not constitute a politically dominant plurality of the total population of a given society. A sociological minority is not necessarily a

Go to Cram101.com for the Practice Tests for this Chapter.

numerical minority it may include any group that is disadvantaged with respect to a dominant group in terms of social status, education, employment, wealth and political power.

Northern Ireland	Northern Ireland has been for many years the site of a violent and bitter ethno-political conflict between those claiming to represent Nationalists, who are predominantly Catholic, and those claiming to represent Unionists, who are predominantly Protestant. In general, Nationalists want Northern Ireland to be unified with the Republic of Ireland, and Unionists want it to remain part of the United Kingdom. Unionists are in the majority in Northern Ireland, though Nationalists represent a significant minority.
Rebellion	A rebellion is, in the most general sense, a refusal to accept authority. It may therefore be seen as encompassing a range of behaviors from civil disobedience to a violent organized attempt to destroy established authority. It is often used in reference to armed resistance against an established government, but can also refer to mass nonviolent resistance movements.
Civil rights	Civil rights are the protections and privileges of personal liberty given to all citizens by law. Civil rights are rights that are bestowed by nations on those within their territorial boundaries.
Civil rights movement	Historically, the civil rights movement was a concentrated period of time around the world of approximately one generation (1954-1980) wherein there was much worldwide civil unrest and popular rebellion.
Diaspora	The dispersal of an ethnic population from an original homeland into foreign areas, often in a forced manner or under traumatic circumstances, is referred to as a diaspora.
Anti-Semitism	Anti-semitism is hostility toward or prejudice against Jews as a religious, racial, or ethnic group, which can range in expression from individual hatred to institutionalized, violent persecution.
Arab-Israeli conflict	The Arab-Israeli conflict involves the establishment of the modern State of Israel, as well as the establishment and independence of several Arab countries at the same time, and the relationship between the Arab nations and Israel. Many countries, individuals and non-governmental organizations elsewhere in the world feel involved in this conflict for reasons such as cultural and religious ties with Islam, Arab culture, Christianity, Judaism or Jewish culture, or for ideological, human rights, strategic or financial reasons.
Islam	Islam is a monotheistic religion originating with the teachings of Muhammad, a 7th-century Arab religious and political figure. Islam includes many religious practices. Adherents are generally required to observe the Five Pillars of Islam, which are five duties that unite Muslims into a community.
Judaism	Judaism is the religion of the Jewish people, based on principles and ethics embodied in the Bible and the Talmud. It is among the oldest religious traditions still in practice today. While Judaism has seldom, if ever, been monolithic in practice, it has always been monotheistic in theology. It differs from many religions in that central authority is not vested in a person or group, but in sacred texts and traditions.
Law of Return	The Law of Return is Israeli legislation, when the memory of World War II and the Holocaust were still fresh, that gives Jews, being those with a Jewish mother or grandmother, or a spouse of such a Jew, or a convert to Judaism the right to migrate to and settle in Israel and gain citizenship.
Muslim	A Muslim is an adherent of the religion of Islam. They believe that there is only one God, translated in Arabic as Allah. They also believe that Islam existed long before Muhammad and that the religion has evolved with time.
Zionism	Zionism is an international political movement that supports a homeland for the Jewish people

Go to **Cram101.com** for the Practice Tests for this Chapter.

	in the Land of Israel. Formally organized in the late 19th century, the movement was successful in establishing the State of Israel in 1948, as the world's first and only modern Jewish State.
Intifada	Intifada is an Arabic word for shaking off, though it is generally translated into English as rebellion.
Arafat, Yasser	Arafat, Yasser was a Palestinian guerrilla soldier and diplomat. The majority of Palestinian, Arab and Islamic people regardless of political ideology or faction viewed him as a heroic freedom fighter and martyr who symbolized the national aspirations of his people. He became ill and fell into a coma. While the exact cause of death remains unknown, doctors spoke of idiopathic thrombocytopenic purpura and cirrhosis. Rumors circulated and continue to that he had been poisoned or succumbed to HIV/AIDS.
Organization	In sociology organization is understood as planned, coordinated and purposeful action of human beings to construct or compile a common tangible or intangible product or service.
Bushmen	The Bushmen are indigenous people of the Kalahari Desert, which spans areas of South Africa, Botswana, Namibia and Angola. They were traditionally hunter-gatherers, part of the Khoisan group, and are related to the traditionally pastoral Khoikhoi. Genetic evidence suggests they are one of the oldest, if not the oldest, peoples in the world.
Khoikhoi	The Khoikhoi are a historical division of the Khoisan ethnic group of southwestern Africa, closely related to the Bushmen. They had lived in southern Africa since the 5th century CE and, at the time of the arrival of white settlers in 1652, practised extensive pastoral agriculture in the Cape region.
National Women's Party	The National Women's Party was a women's organization founded in 1913 that fought for women's rights during the early 20th century in the United States, particularly for the right to vote on the same terms as men and against employment discrimination.
Pass laws	Pass laws in South Africa were designed to segregate the population and limit severely the movements of the non-white populace.
Colonialism	Colonialism is the extension of a nation's sovereignty over territory beyond its borders by the establishment of either settler colonies or administrative dependencies in which indigenous populations are directly ruled or displaced.
Congress	In politics, a congress "a gathering of people" is the name of the main legislative body in a state that operates under a congressional system of government. In non-political usage congress is a term applied to a large national or international grouping of people meeting together with common interests or concerns, e.g. an academic conference.
Nelson Mandela	Nelson Mandela is a former President of South Africa, the first to be elected in fully representative democratic elections. Before his presidency, Mandela was an anti-apartheid activist and leader of the African National Congress and its armed wing Umkhonto we Sizwe. He spent 27 years in prison, much of it on Robben Island, on convictions for crimes that included sabotage committed while he spearheaded the struggle against apartheid.
Peace	Peace is a state of harmony, the absence of hostility. This term is applied to describe a cessation of violent international conflict; in this international context, peace is the opposite of war. Peace can also describe a relationship between any parties characterized by respect, justice, and goodwill.
Taylor	Taylor was an American engineer who sought to improve industrial efficiency. He was one of the intellectual leaders of the Efficiency Movement and his ideas, broadly conceived, were highly influential in the Progressive Era. During the latter part of his career he was a management consultant, and he is sometimes called "The Father of Scientific Management."

Truth	The meaning of the word truth extends from honesty, good faith, and sincerity in general, to agreement with fact or reality in particular. The term has no single definition about which the majority of professional philosophers and scholars agree. Various theories of truth continue to be debated. There are differing claims on such questions as what constitutes truth; how to define and identify truth; the roles that revealed and acquired knowledge play; and whether truth is subjective, relative, objective, or absolute.
Truth and Reconciliation Commission	Truth and reconciliation commission is a commission tasked with discovering and revealing past wrongdoing by a government, in the hope of resolving conflict left over from the past.
William Julius Wilson	William Julius Wilson is an American sociologist. In The Declining Significance of Race: Blacks and Changing American Institutions he argues that the significance of race is waning, and an African-American's class is comparatively more important in determining his or her life chances.
Howard Winant	Howard Winant is an American sociologist and race theorist. Professor Winant is most well known for developing the theory of racial formation along with Michael Omi. Currently, Winant is Professor of Sociology at the University of California, Santa Barbara. Winant's research and teachings revolve around race and racism, comparative historical sociology, political sociology, social theory, and human rights.
Apartheid	Apartheid was a system of racial segregation in South Africa. The rules of Apartheid dictated that people be legally classified into racial groups -- the main ones were Black, White, Coloured and Indian -- and separated from one another on the basis of legal classification and unequal rights.
Kaiser Family Foundation	The Kaiser Family Foundation is a U.S.-based non-profit, private operating foundation headquartered in Menlo Park, California. Its focuses on the major health care issues facing the nation, with a growing role in global health. The Foundation is an independent voice and source of facts and analysis for policymakers, the media, the health care community, and the general public.
South African Institute of Race Relations	The South African Institute of Race Relations is a leading research and policy organization in South Africa. The Institute is "one of the oldest liberal institutions in the country," and is independent of government and all political parties; it sees its role as serving its members and the country at large to make South Africa the political and economic success of the continent by promoting liberal democratic values.
Restitution	The law of restitution is the law of gains-based recovery. When a court orders restitution it orders the defendant to give up his gains to the claimant.
Wine	Wine is an alcoholic beverage made from the fermentation of grape juice. The natural chemical balance of grapes is such that they can ferment without the addition of sugars, acids, enzymes or other nutrients. Wine is produced by fermenting crushed grapes using various types of yeast which consume the sugars found in the grapes and convert them into alcohol. Various varieties of grapes and strains of yeasts are used depending on the types of wine produced.
Michael Wines	Michael Wines is an American journalist who is the South Africa bureau chief for The New York Times, based in Johannesburg. He also covered municipal and state government, politics and education for The Louisville Times.

Melting Pot	The melting pot is a metaphor for the way in which homogeneous societies develop, in which the ingredients in the pot (people of different cultures and religions) are combined so as to lose their discrete identities to some degree, yielding a final product which has a more
Cannabis	Cannabis is a genus of flowering plants that includes three putative species, Cannabis sativa L., Cannabis indica Lam., and Cannabis ruderalis Janisch. These three taxa are indigenous to central Asia and surrounding regions. Cannabis has long been used for fibre, for medicinal purposes, and as a psychoactive.
Israel Zangwill	Israel Zangwill was an English-born humourist and writer. He was also involved in politics as an assimilationist, an early Zionist, a territorialist, a feminist and a pacifist. He wrote a very influential novel Children of the Ghetto: A Study of a Peculiar People. The use of the metaphorical phrase melting pot to describe American absorption of immigrants was popularised by his play The Melting Pot.
Marvin Harris	Marvin Harris was an American anthropologist. A prolific writer, he was highly influential in the development of cultural materialism. In his work he combined Karl Marx's emphasis on the forces of production with Malthus's insights on the impact of demographic factors on other parts of the sociocultural system. Labeling demographic and production factors as infrastructure, Harris posited these factors as key in determining a society's social structure and culture.
Minority	A minority is a sociological group that does not constitute a politically dominant plurality of the total population of a given society. A sociological minority is not necessarily a numerical minority it may include any group that is disadvantaged with respect to a dominant group in terms of social status, education, employment, wealth and political power.
Minority group	A minority group or subordinate group is a sociological group that does not constitute a politically dominant plurality of the total population of a given society.
Old age	Old age consists of ages nearing or surpassing the average life span of human beings, and thus the end of the human life cycle. Some believe there to be prejudice against older people in Western cultures, which is one form of ageism.
Groups	In sociology, a group can be defined as two or more humans that interact with one another, accept expectations and obligations as members of the group, and share a common identity. By this definition, society can be viewed as a large group, though most social groups are considerably smaller.
Population	A population is the collection of people or organisms of a particular species living in a given geographic area or space, usually measured by a census.
Ageing	Ageing is the process of systems' deterioration with time. It is an important part of all human societies reflecting the biological changes that occur, but also reflecting cultural and societal conventions.
Ageism	Ageism refers to prejudice against a person on the grounds of age in the belief that the age category is inferior to other age categories and that unequal treatment is therefore justified.
Age Discrimination in Employment Act	The Age Discrimination in Employment Act prohibits employment discrimination against persons 40 years of age or older in the United States. The law also sets standards for pensions and benefits provided by employers and requires that information about the needs of older workers be provided to the general public.
Committee	A committee is a type of small deliberative assembly that is usually subordinate to another, larger deliberative assembly.
Discrimination	Discrimination refers to the denial of equal access to social resources to people on the

basis of their group membership.

Senate	A senate is a deliberative body, often the upper house or chamber of a legislature.
American Association of Retired Persons	American Association of Retired Persons, is a United States-based non-government organization. According to its mission statement, it is "a nonprofit, nonpartisan membership organization for people age 50 and over ... dedicated to enhancing quality of life for all as we age," which "provides a wide range of unique benefits, special products, and services for our members."
Equal Employment Opportunity Commission	The Equal Employment Opportunity Commission is a United States federal agency tasked with ending employment discrimination in the United States. It also serves as an adjudicatory for claims of discrimination brought against federal agencies.
Conflict theory	Conflict theory emphasizes the role of coercion and power, a person's or group's ability to exercise influence and control over others, in producing social order. It states that a society or organization functions so that each individual participant and its groups struggle to maximize their benefits, which inevitably contributes to social change such as changes in politics and revolutions.
Gray Panthers	Gray Panthers is an American organization promoting senior citizens' rights, founded by Maggie Kuhn in 1970, in response to her forced retirement at age 65.
Medicare	Medicare is a health insurance program administered by the United States government, covering people who are either age 65 and over, or who meet other special criteria. Since the beginning of the Medicare program, CMS has contracted to private companies to assist with administrating the program. These contractors are commonly already in the insurance or health care area.
Security	Security is the condition of being protected against danger or loss.
Social Security	Social security primarily refers to social welfare service concerned with social protection, or protection against socially recognized conditions, including poverty, old age, disability, unemployment and others.
Disability	Disability is lack of ability relative to a personal or group standard or spectrum. Disability may involve physical impairment, sensory impairment, cognitive or intellectual impairment, mental disorder also known as psychiatric disability, or various types of chronic disease. A disability may occur during a person's lifetime or may be present from birth.
Status	In sociology or anthropology, social status is the honor or prestige attached to one's position in society one's social position. The stratification system, which is the system of distributing rewards to the members of society, determines social status. Social status, the position or rank of a person or group within the stratification system, can be determined two ways. One can earn their social status by their own achievements, which is known as achieved status, or one can be placed in the stratification system by their inherited position, which is called ascribed status.
Sears	Sears is an American mid-range chain of international department stores, founded by Richard Sears and Alvah Roebuck in the late 19th century. It operates in Canada under Sears Canada, Mexico under Sears Mexico and Guatemala under Homemart, S.A.
Labeling	Labeling is defining or describing a person in terms of his or her behavior. The term is often used in sociology to describe human interaction, control and identification of deviant behavior.
Asch	Asch was a world-renowned American Gestalt psychologist and pioneer in social psychology. He became famous in the 1950s, following experiments which showed that social pressure can make

a person say something that is obviously incorrect.

Americans with Disabilities Act	The Americans with Disabilities Act is a wide-ranging civil rights law that prohibits, under certain circumstances, discrimination based on disability. It affords similar protections against discrimination to Americans with disabilities as the Civil Rights Act of 1964, which made discrimination based on race, religion, sex, national origin, and other characteristics illegal. Disability is defined as "a physical or mental impairment that substantially limits a major life activity." The determination of whether any particular condition is considered a disability is made on a case by case basis. Certain specific conditions are excluded as disabilities, such as current substance abusers.
Berkeley Center for Independent Living	The Berkeley Center for Independent Living is the world's first organization managed by people with disabilities and is a national leader in supporting disabled people in their efforts to lead independent lives. It provides free services and referrals that guide people through systems such as the housing and employment market.
Disabled in Action	Disabled in Action is a civil rights organization, based in New York City, committed to ending discrimination against people with disabilities. It is involved with The One Step Campaign, a coalition of disability, advocacy and service organizations. The campaign encourages stores, restaurants and other places of public accommodation in the New York City area to provide wheelchair accessibility.
Independent	The independent variables are those that are deliberately manipulated to invoke a change in the dependent variables. In short, "if x is given, then y occurs", where x represents the independent variables and y represents the dependent variables.
National Federation of the Blind	The National Federation of the Blind is an organization of blind people in the United States.
Scotch	Scotch is an alcoholic drink that is made in Scotland. In Britain, the term whisky is usually taken to mean Scotch unless otherwise specified.
Gay	Gay usually describes a person's sexual orientation, being the standard term for homosexual. Gay sometimes also refers to commonalities shared by homosexual people, as in "gay history", the ideological concept of a hypothetical gay culture, as in "gay music." The word gay is sometimes used to refer to same-sex relationships.
Gene	A gene is a locatable region of genomic sequence, corresponding to a unit of inheritance, which is associated with regulatory regions, transcribed regions and/or other functional sequence regions. A gene is a union of genomic sequences encoding a coherent set of potentially overlapping functional products.
Lesbian	A lesbian is a woman who is romantically and sexually attracted only to other women. Some women in same-sex relationships do not identify as lesbian, but as bisexual, queer, or another label. As with any interpersonal activity, sexual expression depends on the context of the relationship.
Alfred Kinsey	Alfred Kinsey was an American biologist and professor of entomology and zoology who founded the Institute for Research in Sex, Gender and Reproduction at Indiana University, now called the Kinsey Institute for Research in Sex, Gender and Reproduction. His research on human sexuality profoundly influenced social and cultural values in the United States and many other countries.
Voter News Service	The Voter News Service was a consortium whose mission was to provide results for United States Presidential elections, so that individual organizations and networks would not have to do exit polling and vote tallying in parallel.
Student	A student could be described as 'one who directs zeal at a subject'.

Cloud	A cloud is a visible mass of droplets or frozen crystals floating in the atmosphere above the surface of the Earth or another planetary body.
Coalition	A coalition is an alliance among entities, during which they cooperate in joint action, each in their own self-interest. This alliance may be temporary or a matter of convenience. A coalition thus differs from a more formal covenant.
Homophobia	Homophobia is a term used to describe irrational fear of, aversion to, or discrimination against homosexuals. It can also mean "irrational fear of, aversion to, or discrimination against homosexuality or homosexuals". Homophobic is the adjective form of this term used to describe the qualities of these characteristics while homophobe is the noun form given as a title to individuals with homophobic characteristics.
Harvey Milk	Harvey Milk was an American politician and gay rights activist, and the first openly gay city supervisor of San Francisco, California. He was, according to Time magazine, "the first openly gay man elected to any substantial political office in the history of the planet." He was assassinated by Dan White, making him a LGBT community "martyr".
National Coalition of Anti-Violence Programs	The National Coalition of Anti-Violence Programs is a national organization dedicated to reducing violence and its impacts on lesbian, gay, bisexual and transgender individuals in the U.S.A.
Power	Power is the ability of a person to control or influence the choices of other persons. The term authority is often used for power perceived as legitimate by the social structure. Power can be seen as evil or unjust; indeed all evil and injustice committed by man against man involve power.
Epidemic	In epidemiology, an epidemic is a disease that appears as new cases in a given human population, during a given period, at a rate that substantially exceeds what is "expected", based on recent experience
Prejudice	Prejudice is, as the name implies, the process of "pre-judging" something. It implies coming to a judgment on a subject before learning where the preponderance of evidence actually lies, or forming a judgment without direct experience.
Bowers v. Hardwick	Bowers v. Hardwick was a United States Supreme Court decision that upheld the constitutionality of a Georgia sodomy law that criminalized oral and anal sex in private between consenting adults.
Bill Clinton	Bill Clinton was the forty-second President of the United States. He presided over the longest period of peace-time economic expansion in American history, which included a balanced budget and a federal surplus. His first term saw the passage of economic legislation.
Linda Greenhouse	Linda Greenhouse a Pulitzer Prize winning reporter who covered the United States Supreme Court for three decades for the The New York Times. She has also faced criticism for expressing publicly, her personal views supporting abortion rights and criticism of US policies and actions at Guantanamo Bay, Abu Ghraib, and Haditha.
Laud Humphreys	Laud Humphreys was an American sociologist and author. He best known for his published Ph.D. dissertation, Tearoom Trade, an ethnographic study of anonymous male-male sexual encounters in public toilets. He asserted that the men participating in such activity came from diverse social backgrounds, had differing personal motives for seeking homosexual contact in such venues, and variously self-perceived as "straight," "bisexual," or "gay."
Justice	Justice concerns the proper ordering of things and persons within a society. As a concept it has been subject to philosophical, legal, and theological reflection and debate throughout history.

Lawrence v. Texas	Lawrence v. Texas was a landmark United States Supreme Court case. In the 6-3 ruling, the justices struck down the sodomy law in Texas. It explicitly overruled Bowers, holding that it had viewed the liberty interest too narrowly. Its outcome was celebrated by gay rights advocates, who hoped that further legal advances might result as a consequence. Conversely, it was decried by social conservatives as an example of judicial activism.
Stonewall Inn	The Stonewall Inn was the site of the famous Stonewall riots of 1969, which have come to symbolize the beginning of the gay liberation movement in the United States.
Policy	A policy is a deliberate plan of action to guide decisions and achieve rational outcomes. The term may apply to government, private sector organizations and groups, and individuals. Presidential executive orders, corporate privacy policies, and parliamentary rules of order are all examples of policy. Policy differs from rules or law. While law can compel or prohibit behaviors policy merely guides actions toward those that are most likely to achieve a desired outcome.
Defense of Marriage Act	The Defense of Marriage Act is the short title of a federal law of the United States passed on September 21, 1996 as Public Law No. 104-199, 110 Stat. 2419. Its provisions are codified at 1 U.S.C. § 7 and 28 U.S.C. § ^{1738}C. The law has two effects: 1) No state need treat a relationship between persons of the same sex as a marriage, even if the relationship is considered a marriage in another state, and 2) The Federal Government may not treat same-sex relationships as marriages for any purpose, even if concluded or recognized by one of the states.
Domestic partnership	A household partnership in which an unmarried couple lives together in a committed, sexually intimate relationship and is granted the same benefits as those accorded to married heterosexual couples is a domestic partnership.
Marriage	A marriage is an interpersonal relationship with governmental, social, or religious recognition, usually intimate and sexual, and often created as a contract. The most frequently occurring form of marriage unites a man and a woman as husband and wife. Other forms of marriage also exist; for example, polygamy, in which a person takes more than one spouse, is common in many societies
Partnership	A partnership is a type of business entity in which partners share with each other the profits or losses of the business undertaking in which all have invested.
African Americans	African Americans are citizens or residents of the United States whose ancestors, usually in predominant part, were indigenous to Sub-Saharan Africa. Most are the descendants of captive Africans who were enslaved within the boundaries of the present United States.
Hispanic	Hispanic is a term that historically denoted relation to the ancient Hispania and its peoples. The term now refers to the culture and people of the Spanish-speaking countries of Hispanic America and Spain; or countries with a historical legacy from Spain, including the Southwestern United States and Florida; the African nations of Equatorial Guinea, Western Sahara and the Northern coastal region of Morocco; the Asia-Pacific nations of the Philippines, Guam, Northern Mariana Islands; and to the ethnic individuals of those cultures. It can also refer to the Hispanosphere geographical distribution, the same way Latin refers to the Romance languages in general.
Hispanic American	Hispanic American is an American citizen or resident of Hispanic ethnicity and can identify themselves as having Hispanic Cultural heritage. According to the 2000 Census, Hispanics constitute the second largest ethnic group in the United States, compromizing roughly 12.5% of the population.
Life expectancy	The number of years a newborn in a particular society can expect to live is referred to as a life expectancy.

Go to **Cram101.com** for the Practice Tests for this Chapter.

Income	Income, generally defined, is the money that is received as a result of the normal business activities of an individual or a business.
John F. Kennedy	John F. Kennedy was the thirty-fifth President of the United States, serving from 1961 until his assassination in 1963.
Absolute deprivation	A lack of basic necessities relative to a fixed standard such as the amount of food necessary for survival is referred to as absolute deprivation.
Affirmative action	Affirmative action refers to policies intended to promote access to education or employment aimed at a historically socio-politically non-dominant group. Motivation for affirmative action policies is to redress the effects of past discrimination and to encourage public institutions such as universities, hospitals and police forces to be more representative of the population.
Amalgamation	Amalgamation is a now largely archaic term for the intermarriage and interbreeding of different ethnicities or races. In the English-speaking world, the term has been in use into the twentieth century. In the United States, it was partly replaced after 1863 by the term miscegenation. While the term amalgamation could refer to the interbreeding of different white as well as non-white ethnicities, the term miscegenation was used to refer specifically to the interbreeding of whites and non-whites, especially African-Americans.[1]
Androgyny	Androgyny refers to the blending of traditional feminine and masculine traits.
Apartheid	Apartheid was a system of racial segregation in South Africa. The rules of Apartheid dictated that people be legally classified into racial groups -- the main ones were Black, White, Coloured and Indian -- and separated from one another on the basis of legal classification and unequal rights.
Authoritarianism	Authoritarianism describes a form of government characterized by strict obedience to the authority of the state, which often maintains and enforces social control through the use of oppressive measures. The term may also be used to describe the personality or management style of an individual or organization which seeks to dominate those within its sphere of influence and has little regard for building consensus.
Authoritarian personality	A set of distinctive personality traits, including conformity, intolerance, and an inability to accept ambiguity, is referred to as an authoritarian personality.
Brain	In animals, the brain is the control center of the central nervous system, responsible for behavior. In mammals, the brain is located in the head, protected by the skull and close to the primary sensory apparatus of vision, hearing, equilibrioception, sense of taste, and olfaction.
Brain drain	Brain drain refers to the persistent loss of the most capable people of a country or region, especially their young people, by emigration due to the lure of opportunities and benefits elsewhere.
Chicanismo	Chicanismo is a cultural movement begun in the 1930s in the Southwestern United States by Mexican Americans to recapture their Mexican, Native American culture.
Civil Disobedience	Civil disobedience encompasses the active refusal to obey certain laws, demands and commands of a government or of an occupying power without resorting to physical violence.
Civil religion	In the sociology of religion, civil religion is the folk religion of a nation or a political culture. Professional commentators on political and social matters sometimes use the term civil religion to refer to ritual expressions of patriotism of a sort practiced in all countries, not always including religion in the conventional sense of the word.
Colonialism	Colonialism is the extension of a nation's sovereignty over territory beyond its borders by the establishment of either settler colonies or administrative dependencies in which

indigenous populations are directly ruled or displaced.

Comparable worth	The evaluation of jobs dominated by women and those traditionally dominated by men on the basis of training, skills, and experience in attempts to equalize wage is referred to as comparable worth.
Conflict perspective	A theoretical perspective that focuses on the struggle among different social groups over scarce resources is referred to as conflict perspective or conflict theory.
Contact	In Family Law, contact is one of the general terms which denotes the level of contact a parent or other significant person in a child's life can have with that child. Contact forms part of the bundle of rights and privileges which a parent may have in relation to any child of the family.
Contact hypothesis	The notion that prejudice can be reduced through increased contact among members of different social groups is referred to as contact hypothesis.
Culture	Culture generally refers to patterns of human activity and the symbolic structures that give such activity significant importance. Culture has been called "the way of life for an entire society." As such, it includes codes of manners, dress, language, religion, rituals, norms of behavior such as law and morality, and systems of belief.
Culture of poverty	The culture of poverty concept is a social theory explaining the cycle of poverty. Based on the concept that the poor have a unique value system, the culture of poverty theory suggests the poor remain in poverty because of their adaptations to the burdens of poverty.
Culture-of-poverty theory	Culture-of-poverty theory is a social theory explaining the cycle of poverty. Based on the concept that the poor have a unique value system, it suggests the poor remain in poverty because of their adaptations to the burdens of poverty.
Curanderismo	Curanderismo is a holistic system of Latin American folk medicine. It blends religious beliefs, faith, and prayer eith the use of herbs, massage, and other traditional methods of healing. It is used to treat ailments arising from physical, psychological, spiritual, or social conditions.
Pay equity	Pay equity is a method of eliminating discrimination against women who are paid less than men for jobs requiring comparable levels of expertise. A policy to establish pay equity usuallys refers to that all jobs will be evaluated and given points according to the level of knowledge and responsibility required to do the job and that salary adjustments will be made if its discovered that women are consistently paid less then men for jobs with similar points.
Racism	Racism, by its simplest definition, is discrimination based on race. People with racist beliefs might hate certain groups of people according to their race, or in the case of institutional racism, certain racial groups may be denied rights or benefits. Racism typically starts with the assumption that there are taxonomic differences between different groups of people. According to the United Nations conventions, there is no distinction between the term racial discrimination and ethnic discrimination.
Equity	Equity is the concept or idea of fairness in economics, particularly as to taxation or welfare economics.
Hypothesis	A hypothesis consists either of a suggested explanation for a phenomenon or of a reasoned proposal suggesting a possible correlation between multiple phenomena. The term derives from the Greek, hypotithenai meaning "to put under" or "to suppose." The scientific method requires that one can test a scientific hypothesis. Scientists generally base such hypotheses on previous observations or on extensions of scientific theories. Even though the words "hypothesis" and "theory" are often used synonymously in common and informal usage, a scientific hypothesis is not the same as a scientific theory.

Identity	Identity is an umbrella term used throughout the social sciences to describe an individual's comprehension of him or herself as a discrete, separate entity.
Personality	In psychology, personality is a description of consistent emotional, thought, and behavior patterns in a person. The several theoretical perspectives on personality involve different ideas about the relationship between personality and other psychological constructs as well as different ideas about the way personality doesn't develop.
Poverty	Poverty may be seen as the collective condition of poor people, or of poor groups, and in this sense entire nation-states are sometimes regarded as poor. Although the most severe poverty is in the developing world, there is evidence of poverty in every region.
Race	The term race refers to the concept of dividing people into populations or groups on the basis of various sets of characteristics and beliefs about common ancestry. The most widely used human racial categories are based on visible traits especially skin color, facial features and hair texture, and self-identification.
Religion	A religion is a set of common beliefs and practices generally held by a group of people, often codified as prayer, ritual, and religious law. Religion also encompasses ancestral or cultural traditions, writings, history, and mythology, as well as personal faith and mystic experience.
De facto	De facto is a Latin expression that means "in fact" or "in practice" but not spelled out by law. The term de facto may also be used when there is no relevant law or standard, but a common practice is well established, although perhaps not quite universal. A de facto standard is a technical or other standard that is so dominant that everybody seems to follow it like an authorized standard.
De facto segregation	Segregation that is an unintended consequence of social or ecological arrangements is referred to as de facto segregation.
De jure	De jure is an expression that means "based on law". The phrase is often used in the context of American desegregation legislation. Codified segregation is de jure segregation.
De jure segregation	De jure segregation in both South Africa and the U.S. came with "miscegenation laws" (prohibitions against interracial marriage) and laws against hiring people of the race that is the object of discrimination in any but menial positions.
Denomination	The third most powerful type of religious institution, with a membership generally dominated by a single social class, a formal but not bureaucratic role structure, a trained clergy, traditional authority, abstract relatively unemotional ritual, and a condition of coexistence between it and dominant political and economic institutions, is referred to as a denomination.
Diaspora	The dispersal of an ethnic population from an original homeland into foreign areas, often in a forced manner or under traumatic circumstances, is referred to as a diaspora.
Dysfunction	Dysfunction refers to an institution's negative impact on the sociocultural system.
Emigration	Emigration is the act and the phenomenon of leaving one's native country to settle abroad.
Environmental justice	Environmental justice is a term in the social sciences used to describe injustices in the way natural resources are used. Environmental justice is a holistic effort to analyze and overcome the power structures that have traditionally thwarted environmental reforms.
Ethnic cleansing	Ethnic cleansing refers to the creation of ethnically homogeneous territories through the mass expulsion of other ethnic populations.
Ethnocentrism	Ethnocentrism is the tendency to look at the world primarily from the perspective of one's own culture. It often entails the belief that one's own race or ethnic group is the most

important and/or that some or all aspects of its culture are superior to those of other groups.

Exploitation	In political economy, economics, and sociology, exploitation involves a persistent social relationship in which certain persons are being mistreated or unfairly used for the benefit of others. This corresponds to one ethical conception of exploitation, that is, the treatment of human beings as mere means to an end — or as mere "objects".
Family of Love	The Family of Love were a mystic religious sect known as the Familia Caritatis, founded by Hendrik Niclaes.
Feminine mystique	The Feminine Mystique is a 1963 book written by Betty Friedan which attacked the popular notion that women of that time could only find fulfillment through childbearing and homemaking. According to The New York Times obituary of Friedan in 2006, it "ignited the contemporary women's movement in 1963 and as a result permanently transformed the social fabric of the United States and countries around the world" and "is widely regarded as one of the most influential nonfiction books of the 20th century."
Feminization	The term feminization has been used to describe a shift in gender roles and sex roles in a society.
Feminization of poverty	The feminization of poverty has been observed since 1970 as female headed households accounted for a growing proportion of those below the poverty line. A large majority of these women are divorced or never-married mothers.
Functionalism	In the social sciences, specifically sociology and sociocultural anthropology, functionalism is a sociological paradigm that originally attempted to explain social institutions as collective means to fill individual biological needs.
Functionalist perspective	Functionalist perspective is a sociological viewpoint that argues that social inequality is necessary for the survival of any society or for any small or large organization. It is argued that without this inequality, division labor would be difficult.
Gender	Gender refers to the differences between men and women. Gender identity is an individual's self-conception as being male or female, as distinguished from actual biological sex. In general, gender often refers to purely social rather than biological differences.
Gender role	A gender role is a set of perceived behavioral norms associated particularly with males or females, in a given social group or system.
Genocide	Genocide is the deliberate and systematic destruction of an ethnic, religious or national group. It is define as "any of the following acts committed with intent to destroy, in whole or in part, a national, ethnical, racial or religious group, as such: killing members of the group; causing serious bodily or mental harm to members of the group; deliberately inflicting on the group conditions of life, calculated to bring about its physical destruction in whole or in part; imposing measures intended to prevent births within the group; forcibly transferring children of the group to another group."
Gerrymandering	Gerrymandering is a form of redistricting in which electoral district or constituency boundaries are manipulated for an electoral advantage. Gerrymandering may be used to advantage or disadvantage particular constituents, such as members of a racial, linguistic, religious or class group, often in the favor of ruling incumbents or a specific political party.
Glass escalator	The term glass elevator or glass escalator is used to describe the rapid promotion of men over women, especially into management, in female-dominated fields like nursing.
Globalization	Globalization refers to increasing global connectivity, integration and interdependence in the economic, social, technological, cultural, political, and ecological spheres. It is a

Go to **Cram101.com** for the Practice Tests for this Chapter.

	unitary process inclusive of many sub-processes that are increasingly binding people and the biosphere more tightly into one global system.
Hajj	The Hajj is a pilgrimage to Mecca. It is the largest annual pilgrimage in the world. It is the fifth pillar of Islam, an obligation that must be carried out at least once in their lifetime by every able-bodied Muslim who can afford to do so. It is a demonstration of the solidarity of the Muslim people, and their submission to the Arabic god Allah.
Ethnic identity	Ethnic identity refers to an enduring, basic aspect of the self that includes a sense of membership in an ethnic group and the attitudes and feelings related to that membership. Ethnic identity can vary with changes in social context.
Homemaker	Homemaker is a mainly American term which may refer either to: 1) the person within a family who is primarily concerned with the management of the household, whether or not he or she works outside the home, or; 2) a person whose prime occupation is to care for their family and/or home.
Labor	In economics, labor is a measure of the work done by human beings. It is conventionally contrasted with such other factors of production as land and capital. There are theories which have created a concept called human capital, although there are also counter posing macro-economic system theories that think human capital is a contradiction in terms.
Market	A market is a social arrangement that allows buyers and sellers to discover information and carry out a voluntary exchange of goods or services. It is one of the two key institutions that organize trade, along with the right to own property.
Paradox	A paradox can be an apparently true statement or group of statements that leads to a contradiction or a situation which defies intuition; or it can be, seemingly opposite, an apparent contradiction that actually expresses a non-dual truth.
Social role	A social role is a set of connected behaviors, rights and obligations as conceptualized by actors in a social situation. It is mostly defined as an expected behavior in a given individual social status and social position.
Segregation	Segregation may be mandated by law or exist through social norms. Segregation may be maintained by means ranging from discrimination in hiring and in the rental and sale of housing to certain races to vigilante violence such as lynchings; a situation that arises when members of different races mutually prefer to associate and do business with members of their own race would usually be described as separation or de facto separation of the races rather than segregation.
Crow	The Crow are a tribe of Native Americans who historically lived in the Yellowstone River valley and now live on a reservation south of Billings, Montana. Traditional clothing the Crow wore depended on gender. Women tended to wear simple clothes. Male clothing usually consisted of a shirt, trimmed leggings with a belt, a robe, and moccasins. Women held a very significant role within the tribe.
Holocaust	The Holocaust is the term generally used to describe the killing of approximately six million European Jews during World War II, as part of a program of deliberate extermination planned and executed by the National Socialist regime in Germany led by Adolf Hitler.
In-group	In sociology, an in-group is a social group towards which an individual feels loyalty and respect, usually due to membership in the group.
Informal economy	In economics, the term informal economy refers to the general market income category (or sector) wherein certain types of income and the means of their generation are "unregulated by the institutions of society, in a legal and social environment in which similar activities are regulated."

Go to **Cram101.com** for the Practice Tests for this Chapter.

Intelligence	Intelligence is a property of mind that encompasses many related abilities, such as the capacities to reason, to plan, to solve problems, to think abstractly, to comprehend ideas, to use language, and to learn. In some cases, intelligence may include traits such as: creativity, personality, character, knowledge, or wisdom.
Internal colonialism	Internal Colonialism refers to political and economic inequalities between regions within a single society. The term may be used to describe the uneven effects of state development on a regional basis and to describe the exploitation of minority groups within the wider society.
Intifada	Intifada is an Arabic word for shaking off, though it is generally translated into English as rebellion.
Issei	Issei is a term used in countries in North and South America to specify Japanese people who emigrated to other countries in the years preceding World War II. The term issei Japanese American refers specifically to issei living in the United States.
Jihad	Jihad is a religious duty of Muslims. In Arabic, Jihad means "strive" or "struggle". According to scholar John Esposito, Jihad requires Muslims to "struggle in the way of God" or "to struggle to improve one's self and/or society."
Jim Crow laws	The Jim Crow Laws were state and local laws enacted in the Southern and border states of the United States. They mandated "separate but equal" status for black Americans. In reality, this led to treatment and accommodations that were almost always inferior to those provided to white Americans.
Kibei	Kibei was a term often used in the 1940s to describe Japanese Americans born in the United States who returned to America after receiving their education in Japan.
La Raza	La Raza is sometimes used to denote people of the Latino and Chicano world, as well by Mestizos who share the pride of their Native American or national Hispanic heritage. Nonetheless, the term and idea associated with it have been mainly adopted by some Mexican people in the United States to express pride in their nation.
Labeling theory	A social theory that holds that society's reaction to certain behaviors is a major factor in defining the self as deviant is labeling theory.
Life chances	Life chances are the opportunities each individual has to improve their quality of life. The concept was introduced by German sociologist Max Weber. It is a probabilistic concept, describing how likely it is, given certain factors, that an individual's life will turn out a certain way.
Maquiladora	A maquiladora is a factory that imports materials and equipment on a duty-free and tariff-free basis for assembly or manufacturing and then re-exports the assembled product, usually back to the originating country.
Marielita	Marielita is a term applied to roughly 125,000 people who fled to the United States from the Cuban port of Mariel as part of the exodus of refugees in 1980.
Migration	The movement of people from one country or region to another in order to settle permanently, is referred to as a migration.
Model minority	Model minority refers to a minority ethnic, racial, or religious group whose members achieve a higher degree of success than the population average. This success is typically measured in income, education, and related factors such as low crime rate and high family stability.
Mojados	Mojados is a municipality located in the province of Valladolid, Castile and León, Spain.
Mommy track	Mommy track is a term used to describe the lifestyle of women who choose to leave the workforce in order to pursue childbearing. This is a source of considerable political and social discussion.

Go to **Cram101.com** for the Practice Tests for this Chapter.

Nativism	Although opposition to immigration is a feature of all countries with immigration, the term nativism originated in American politics and has a specific meaning. Strictly speaking, the term nativism distinguishes between Americans who were born in the United States, and individuals who have immigrated - 'first generation' immigrants.
Naturalization	The origin of the term naturalization is that it gives to a resident alien almost all of the rights held by a natural-born citizen.
Normative	In social sciences the term normative is used to describe the effects of those structures of culture which regulate the function of social activity. Those structures thus act to encourage or enforce social activity and outcomes that ought to occur, while discouraging or preventing social activity that ought not occur.
Northern Ireland	Northern Ireland has been for many years the site of a violent and bitter ethno-political conflict between those claiming to represent Nationalists, who are predominantly Catholic, and those claiming to represent Unionists, who are predominantly Protestant. In general, Nationalists want Northern Ireland to be unified with the Republic of Ireland, and Unionists want it to remain part of the United Kingdom. Unionists are in the majority in Northern Ireland, though Nationalists represent a significant minority.
Pushout	A pushout is a student counseled or forced out of a school prior to graduation.
Economy	An economy is the system of human activities related to the production, distribution, exchange, and consumption of goods and services of a country or other area. The composition of a given economy is inseparable from technological evolution, civilization's history and social organization.
Neocolonialism	Neocolonialism is a term used by some intellectuals to describe international economic arrangements by which former colonial powers maintained control of their former colonies and new dependencies following World War II.
Nisei	Nisei are people, or a person, of Japanese ancestry and the first generation to be born abroad.
Orientalism	Orientalism refers to the imitation or depiction of aspects of Eastern cultures in the West by writers, designers and artists, and can also refer to a sympathetic stance towards the region by a writer or other person.
Pan-Indianism	Pan-Indianism is an intertribal movement of native resistance to white domination and assimilation. It is characterized primarily by political and religious expressions and solidarity. Key historical figures incldue Pontiac and Handsome Lake. Pan-Indianism is a non-violent liberation philosophy with roots in Native.
Pass laws	Pass laws in South Africa were designed to segregate the population and limit severely the movements of the non-white populace.
Pluralism	Pluralism is, in the general sense, the affirmation and acceptance of diversity. Pluralism is connected with the hope that this process of conflict and dialogue will lead to a definition and subsequent realization of the common good that is best for all members of society.
Racial formation	Racial formation is an analytical theory developed by Michael Omi and Howard Winant which is used to look at race as a socially constructed identity, where the content and importance of racial categories is determined by social, economic, and political forces. Unlike other traditional race theories, In Omi and Winant's view, racial meanings pervade US society, extending from the shaping of individual racial identities to the structuring of collective political action on the terrain of the state.
Redlining	Redlining is the practice of denying or increasing the cost of services, such as banking, insurance, access to jobs, access to health care, or even supermarkets to residents in

Go to **Cram101.com** for the Practice Tests for this Chapter.

certain, often racially determined, areas. The most devastating form of redlining, and the most common use of the term, refers to mortgage discrimination, in which middle-income black and Hispanic residents are denied loans that are made available to lower-income whites.

Refugee

According to the 1951 United Nations Convention Relating to the Status of a Refugee, a refugee is a person who owing to a well-founded fear of being persecuted for reasons of race, religion, nationality, membership of a particular social group, or political opinion, is outside the country of their nationality, and is unable to or, owing to such fear, is unwilling to avail him/herself of the protection of that country.

Restrictive covenant

A restrictive covenant is a legal obligation imposed in a deed by the seller upon the buyer of real estate to do or not to do something. Such restrictions frequently "run with the land" and are enforceable on subsequent buyers of the property. Some are very simple and are meant only to protect a neighborhood from homeowners destroying trees or historic things or otherwise directly harming property values.

Sansei

Sansei is a term used in North and South America to specify the child of a Nisei couple.

Scapegoating

Blaming, punishing, or stigmatizing a relatively powerless individual or group for wrongs that were not of their doing, is referred to as scapegoating.

Shift work

Shift work is an employment practice designed to make use of the 24 hours of the clock, rather than a standard working day. The term shift work includes both long-term night shifts and work schedules in which employees change or rotate shifts.

Self-fulfilling prophecy

A self-fulfilling prophecy is a prediction that directly or indirectly causes itself to become true. Sociologist Robert K. Merton who is credited with coining the expression "self-fulfilling prophecy" and formalizing its structure and consequences. He gives as a feature of the self-fulfilling prophecy: The self-fulfilling prophecy is, in the beginning, a true definition of the situation evoking a new behavior which makes the original false conception come 'true'.

Sexism

Sexism is commonly considered to be discrimination and/or hatred against people based on their sex rather than their individual merits, but can also refer to any and all systemic differentiations based on the sex of the individuals.

Sexual harassment

Sexual harassment refers to the making of persistent unwanted sexual advances by one individual towards another.

Harassment

Harassment refers to a wide spectrum of offensive behavior. When the term is used in a legal sense it refers to behaviors that are found threatening or disturbing, and beyond those that are sanctioned by society. Sexual harassment refers to persistent and unwanted sexual advances, typically in the workplace, where the consequences of refusing are potentially very disadvantaging to the victim.

Interest

Interest is a fee paid on borrowed assets. By far the most common form these assets are lent in is money, but other assets may be lent to the borrower, such as shares, consumer goods through hire purchase, major assets such as aircraft, and even entire factories in finance lease arrangements. In each case the interest is calculated upon the value of the assets in the same manner as upon money.

Vice

Vice is a practice or habit that is considered immoral, depraved, and/or degrading in the associated society.

Social distance

Social distance describes the distance between different groups of society and is opposed to locational distance. The notion includes all differences such as social class, race/ethnicity or sexuality, but also the fact that the different groups do not mix. The term is often applied in cities, but its use is not limited to that.

Sovereignty	Sovereignty is the exclusive right to exercise supreme political (e.g. legislative, judicial, and/or executive) authority over a geographic region, group of people, or oneself.
Symbolic ethnicity	Ethnic identity that is retained only for symbolic importance is a symbolic ethnicity.
Tongs	Tongs are similar to triads except that they originated among the early immigrant Chinatown communities rather than an extention of a modern triad in China. The first tongs formed in the second half of the 19th century among the more marginalized members of early immigrant Chinese American communities for mutual support and protection from white racists.
Tracking	Tracking is the practice, in education, of placing students into different groups within a school, based on academic abilities. For years, schools in the United States and Great Britain have used tracking as a way of dividing students into different "tracks" to facilitate learning. Though the terms "tracking" and "ability grouping" are often used interchangeably, Gamoran 1992 differentiates between the two. He uses the term "tracking" to describe the manner by which students are separated into groups for all academic subjects, but "ability grouping," on the other hand, is the within-class separation of students into groups, based on academic ability. High ability groups are often assigned special work that is more advanced than that of the other students in the class.
Transnationalism	Transnationalism is a social movement grown out of the heightened interconnectivity between people all around the world and the loosening of boundaries between countries.
Underemployment	A condition of having to work part-time when full-time work is desired and sought after is an underemployment.
Underground economy	The underground economy consists of all commerce on which applicable taxes are being evaded. The market includes not only legally-prohibited commerce, but also trade in legal goods and services because some income is not reported and consequently taxation is evaded, e.g., through money laundering, payment in cash, or other means.
Victimology	Victimology is the study of why certain people are victims of crime and how lifestyles affect the chances that a certain person will fall victim to a crime. The field can cover a wide number of disciplines, including sociology, psychology, criminal justice, law and advocacy.
Victimization surveys	Victimization surveys attempts to bypass the underreporting problem by going directly to the victims. The National Crime Victimization Survey (NCVS) is conducted by the U.S. Bureau of the Census in cooperation with the Bureau of Justice Statistics and the U.S. Department of Justice. The NCVS polls over 50,000 households, totaling over 100,000 individuals, in the United States annually using a multistage sample of housing units. Individuals over 12 years old in selected households are interviewed every six months for about three years.
Xenophobia	Xenophobia is a fear or contempt of foreigners or strangers. The term is typically used to describe fear or dislike of foreigners or in general of people different from one's self.
Yellow peril	Yellow Peril was a color metaphor for race that originated in the late nineteenth century with immigration of Chinese laborers to various Western countries, notably the United States, and later to the Japanese during the mid 20th century due to Japanese military expansion.
Yonsei	Yonsei is a term used in geographic areas outside of Japan to specify the child of at least one Sansei parent.
Zionism	Zionism is an international political movement that supports a homeland for the Jewish people in the Land of Israel. Formally organized in the late 19th century, the movement was successful in establishing the State of Israel in 1948, as the world's first and only modern Jewish State.
Clan	A clan is a group of people united by kinship and descent, which is defined by perceived

Go to **Cram101.com** for the Practice Tests for this Chapter.

Go to **Cram101.com** for the Practice Tests for this Chapter.
And, **NEVER** highlight a book again!

descent from a common ancestor found in many pre-industrial societies.

Ethnicity

Ethnicity is a population of human beings whose members identify with each other, either on the basis of a presumed common genealogy or ancestry or recognition by others as a distinct group, or by common cultural, linguistic, religious, or physical traits. The sociologist Max Weber once remarked that "The whole conception of it is so complex and so vague that it might be good to abandon it altogether."

Go to **Cram101.com** for the Practice Tests for this Chapter.

Printed in the United States
212313BV00005B/1/P